ENHANCING
THINKING AND CREATIVITY
WITH
FUTURES STUDIES

by
Charles E. Whaley

Trillium Press
Unionville, New York
Toronto, Ontario

Acknowledgements

There are always many people to thank for bringing a book to publication. Although it is impossible to mention everyone, some key individuals closely related to the evolution of this book must be thanked in print. It is a small attempt to repay the time they have given, their helpful advice, and their keen insights.

First, I would like to thank the faculty of the Futures Studies Program at the University of Houston/Clear Lake for information and advice which continues to grow daily.

There are two individuals who must be thanked publically for taking the time to review, edit, and offer several valuable perspectives. The first is Dr. Jacqueline Robertson of Ball State University who's editing, advice, readability checks, and general support added a great deal to this book. The second is Ms. Marsha Allington, a political consultant based in Indiana who must be thanked not only for her excellent editing, but also for her support and advice.

A special thanks goes to the Futures Studies class members of the 1989 and 1990 Florida Governor's Summer College. Their sharing of their unique perspectives on themselves and the future helped clarify my thinking a great deal.

Trillium Press
First Avenue
Unionville, NY 10988
(914) 726-4444
FAX: (914) 726-3824

Trillium Press
78 Biddeford Ave
Downsview, Ontario
M3H 1K4 Canada
FAX: (416) 633-3010

Printed in the United States of America by the Royal Fireworks Press of Unionville, New York.

ISBN: 0-89824-615-6

ENHANCING THINKING AND CREATIVITY WITH FUTURES STUDIES

TABLE OF CONTENTS

SECTION V: INDEPENDENT STUDY

SECTION VI: THIRTY FUTURES ACTIVITIES FOR THE CLASSROOM

"Scenario: 2030 A.D.: The Recycling Rebound"

SECTION VII: REFERENCES

INTRODUCTION

Smokestacks versus satellites — the slowly fading uniformity of a mass society and the emerging information society with its unprecedented diversity of choices. These emerging options will continue to redefine day-to-day life. The ultimate winners or losers, our children, will spend their adulthood in a society difficult for most of us to recognize.

Futures Studies is really a course in developing one's thinking skills and creativity. The "futures" element focuses a student's skills and abilities on several open-ended issues which will be resolved in the future. Most, if not all, of these issues are certain to influence our personal and mutual futures. Not only do students of futures studies sharpen their thinking skills and creative abilities but they also become more aware of, and familiar with, possible futures — the student becomes more "futures-friendly." What is "futures friendly"? An analogy would be a situation in which you were driving a car at night on a darkened road with no lights. Moving into the future, "without your lights on," darkens the future and makes many occurrences a surprise to which you can only react. With your lights on you are better able to make the needed adjustments sooner, and more important, plan your overall course better. That is "futures friendly" — awareness of options and proacting to create and shape your future.

Regardless of what evolves from the current educational reform movement in the United States, we are at a point where our schools must find a balance in their approach for educating today's students for tomorrow. A balance between the degree of: 1) individualization and standardization of curriculum offered, 2) the specificity and generality of information presented, 3) the variety and routine of classroom activities presented, 4) the breadth and depth of material covered, and finally, 5) a balance between the creativity and conservation promoted in approaching and successfully creating a perspective on one's own future. The study of alternative futures can help curricular and instructional practices become more updated and more suitable for education's most basic purpose: preparing individuals for the future. Increasing numbers of schools are using futures studies as a thematic framework, through which several content areas may find a commonality and a new emphasis. Futures constitutes a ready-made topical and thematic area for revitalizing curriculum. The flexible thinking skills and creative abilities gained through such studies focus on exactly the type of skills needed by "citizens of the future."

With all the ambiguity about the future, there are two things we know. First, we know change is predicted as a long-range constant. There is little doubt our country, indeed our world, continues to enter a new era — an era without precedent. The individual with: 1) knowledge about change and how to cope with it, 2) flexibility in his or her thinking and attitudes, and 3) effective problem-solving skills will be at a *distinct advantage.*

The second thing we know about the future is: when a school has no vision of the future, it teaches the past. This is perhaps the sixth element of the balance needs mentioned above. School districts across this country need to balance "the vision" given to students through the curriculum, so that it reflects not only where we have been and currently are, but where we could possibly be going as a nation and world. Futures studies is not the end all, be all. However, futures studies does have cognitive and affective elements which are becoming more and more important to students trying to understand themselves, their world, and more fully realize future possibilities which will impact on both — a skill of critical import during times of rapid change.

THE INCREASING NEED FOR A FUTURES PERSPECTIVE

As educators, we have had the opportunity to hear many university instructors remind us of our charge to prepare students for the future. As our work for a degree winds down and instructors wax philosophical we hear wonderful rhetoric which excites us and reminds us of the much larger picture in which the primary purpose of education is "to prepare students for a meaningful life as a contributing member of our society and world." When? Now? No, the preparation is for some future point on the horizon. Sometimes that point in time is near, sometimes more distant, depending on the age of the student. However, all preparation is oriented toward the future. Even as we find ourselves sitting in the university classroom we acknowledge we are undergoing the work required for a degree for some benefit or reward in the future — a different job, a higher step on the pay scale, maybe a change in careers.

Education is by its very nature future-oriented. Yet we often isolate ourselves and orient our perspectives on education toward the past. Perhaps a haunting quote from one of America's pre-eminent educators would help:

> "From the standpoint of the child, the great waste in the school comes from his inability to utilize the experience he gets outside of school in any complete and free way within the school itself; while, on the other hand, he is unable to apply in daily life what he is learning at school. That is the isolation of the school — its isolation from life." (John Dewey, 1902)

Questions must be asked here: Who can say that the information and knowledge taught in school today is not catalogued and categorized in much the same way today as it was in Dewey's time? Has our society changed since Dewey's day at the turn of the century? Has the *nature* of knowledge changed since the turn of the century? With factual information having a much shorter lifetime in the information age, is it wise to keep the same emphasis on facts or should we balance factual information with the mastery of processes which would be useful throughout life, such as flexible thinking and creative problem-solving? What do we teach to prepare students for the future? Since we don't know exactly what the future will be like, what skills and information might be needed? It is difficult to come up with an explicit content-oriented recipe similar to what we have had in the past. However, we do know that certain skills and abilities will be useful no matter what the future brings.

CURRENT TRENDS IN THE INFORMATION AGE AND THE CHANGING NATURE OF KNOWLEDGE

We do know certain things about the future. The following information represents some forces and current trends in our society that are changing the way we define knowledge. These trends are seen as long term. These forces and trends are growing out of the information age which can perpetuate itself in a way similar to a vicious circle: information creates more knowledge which creates change which creates more information, which creates more knowledge which creates more change. Because of this cyclical nature of the information age and this updated understanding of "knowledge," schooling, specifically curriculum and instruction, is finding itself stuck with an outdated educational recipe. Here are some trends and a glimpse of their impact on curriculum design:

— In the Information Age "factual information" has an increasingly shorter lifetime. Factual information growing from incidents, events, and issues changes daily. Knowledge is becoming less task, subject, and incident specific, and more conceptual.

1

—The principles, concepts, and data from one specialty or subject area are increasingly applicable in other subject areas; A trend toward interdisciplinary and conceptually-based curriculum continues to emerge. (Whaley, 1984)

—The ability to extract knowledge from information and recognize complex patterns and linkages between apparently unrelated data and events will continue to become highly valued abilities.

—Knowledge is becoming more a matter of process than content, more of imagination, interpretation of data and application of that data than simply recall of the data. An expanded definition of READ in the Information Age might be "Rapid Evaluation and Analysis of Data." (LaConte, 1984)

—New "person/high tech tools" partnerships are releasing humans from certain tasks. This partnership with "tools" frees us from certain simple tasks and allows us to concentrate on more complex tasks which the tools cannot do, such as making decisions based on incomplete information and thinking creativity. Acquiring information and knowledge in the future will require the know-how and flexibility to (1) access, (2) understand and, (3) integrate information from a variety of diverse delivery systems, learning environments, and teaching/learning styles.

—A clearer division between training and education has emerged which curriculum must now reflect: Training has become oriented toward one answer, more convergent in nature, and highly compartmentalized. It often involves sequential, often simple, patterns and repetition. Education is more divergent in nature. It is speculative, often involving the creation of alternatives and developing understandings of the ramifications of certain actions and decisions which also includes the development of concern for stakeholders.

—In the Information Age "factual information" has an increasingly shorter lifetime. Factual information growing from situations, events, and issues changes daily if not hourly. Knowledge is becoming less task, subject, and incident specific, and more conceptual.

—A new concept of literacy is emerging as we become more deeply involved with the information age:

> The first element of the "new literacy" focuses on the *productive use of the computer.* More universities are requiring computer literacy as an admission requirement. With the help of computer companies, increasing numbers of higher education institutions are requiring students to have a computer before the end of their first semester on campus.

> The second element of the new literacy is the development of *"media smart."* Development of media smart requires the ability to discriminate between fact, hypothesis, distortion and rumor in various media. This ever-changing media barrage; what Toffler (1981) calls the "info-sphere," will continue to drive the information age. In a democracy, a majority of the populous must have some degree of formal education. If education does not include the development of abilities aimed at becoming "media smart," it will show later at the polls.

> The final element of our new literacy is the *understanding of the nature of systems.* The interdependence of our world grows out of complex natural and man-made systems whose understanding leads to better long-term decision making.

In summary: As a direct result of the above trends, there needs to be an unmistakable and unrelenting push toward conceptually-oriented, interdisciplinary curriculum with an eye toward broadening our understanding of what literacy in the 21st century entails.

Based only upon the above information, our educational system is in need of modifying some of its current practices. It can start in the classroom. The following information represents processes and perspectives which classroom teachers must give to citizens of the future. One easy way to start this task is to choose materials, etc. which deliver, or require of the student:

* Analysis/synthesis/evaluation of information
* Flexibility of thinking and flexibility of attitudes
* Creativity & creative approaches to problem-solving
* Ability to make decisions from incomplete information
* Integration of information from a variety of diverse sources
* Sense of "empowerment" to shape instead of only react to the future

THE INTERACTIVE FUTURES MODEL FOR IMPLEMENTING A FUTURES PERSPECTIVE AN OVERVIEW OF THE MODEL'S COMPONENTS

This section will present the components which comprise the Interactive Futures Model (I.F. Model). The model is helpful in establishing a theme, a specific unit, or an entire course of study focusing on the examination of alternative futures. Before going in-depth, a quick overview of the components and their interconnectedness might be helpful. Let us examine an overview of a curricular approach which allows integration of the different components into a working model.

The Interactive Futures Curricular Model in Section I involves three primary components:

1) A Conceptual Framework,

2) An Interdisciplinary Approach and,

3) Research Methodologies.

Every component interacts to give students the opportunity to explore, discover, and create future possibilities and options. The exploration of futures themes and topics, coupled with higher order thinking skills and creativity, leads to the behavioral outcomes described in the beginning of Section I. Below is a graphic of the I.F. Model for adding a futuristic perspective to a student's education.

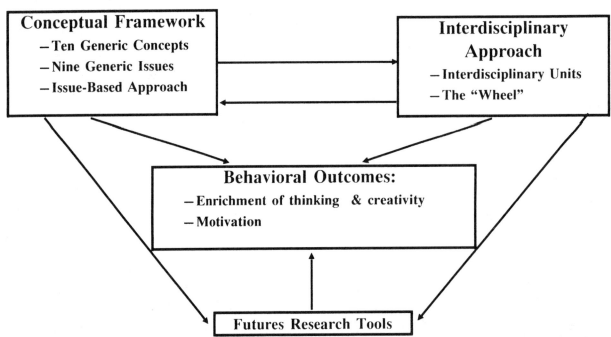

The time given to each of the three components will depend upon the goals and objectives of the teacher. Will the examination of futures studies exist as a class of its own? Will this topical/thematic area provide supplemental information in a traditional class only or is futures studies to serve as a focus for independent study within the framework of social studies, science, mathematics, reading or literature?

The level of information will depend upon the age and ability of the students. If students are young, situations used to illustrate concepts and issues should be more local and concrete. Older, or advanced students, are more open to global and abstract approaches.

4

BEHAVIORAL OUTCOMES: THE REASON BEHIND IT ALL

Behavioral outcomes, the ultimate intent of any intervention or curriculum, is the overall goal of this model. For students to understand better who they are, how the world works, and how possible futures will affect both, is a major step. The other part of this important understanding is to put the new information into action, or new behavioral patterns. To "act" like they know: 1) the actions they take now will affect the future, 2) there are many different futures available, and 3) it is better to shape the future than have it shape you.

All three components of the model combine to enhance the development of skills, attitudes, and flexibility of thinking necessary in the future. The development of more positive and sophisticated, yet realistic, attitudes toward the future is a primary goal. The learning of skills and processes allowing students to shape their future rather than being shaped by it, and learning how to learn in an information age, are also primary outcomes. The goals and objectives later in this section specify the full intent and scope of futures studies.

The Connection Between Student Motivation and Time Orientation

High drop-out rates and low standardized test scores are two problems facing our public school system that give rise to the fear of America will be left behind in the early 21st Century. To better understand why some students achieve to their potential in school and other students fail to do so, educators must examine the connection between the students' time orientation and their resultant levels of motivation. Three basic time orientations exist: past, present, and future. The term time-orientation indicates where an individual images, or sees, him or herself in a temporal sense, and therefore, where they primarily live in time. An individual's time orientation is the result of cultural influence, socio-economic status, educational level, and age. It can change from time to time but one of the three: past-present-future, represents where an individual primarily "lives in time."

We've all heard of individuals who live in the past. Often, this situation reflects a feeling that the best future has already happened. If one's time orientation is toward the past, how does that affect his or her present motivation level(s)? What ramifications does living in the past have in preparing for the future? Would one who lives primarily in the past make plans for a career change or seek further education for some other specific personal goal? Does a person who lives in the past generate any meaningful personal goals oriented toward the future?

Living in the present also has implications for the other two dimensions of time and one's level of motivation. When one lives in the present, with little or no regard for the past or future, plans are all but non-existent. Of the three time orientations, living in the present has the most narrow focus, ranging from a fleeting second to, at most, a few days. More than a few days calls for some degree of planning, indicating the individual is no longer living in the present but also the future.

Within American society there are groups who live only in the present. The poor, the black, and certain immigrant groups are characterized in this way and do, in fact, operate on a time system different from that of the American mainstream. This is reflected in differing attitudes toward punctuality and personal planning. (Singer, 1974) In the most dire situations, the hopelessness and despair of disadvantaged groups in American society lead to a type of timelessness in which the past and future are discounted and the present is the only known. In situations where the deprived are faced with a future that is uncertain, the present expands. Frequently, fate rather than the setting of personal goals and developing one's skills and abilities, determines who and what a person will become. This perspective can be, and is, passed on to students in the home.

The motivating images of self-in-the-future spring from an individual's time orientation. The image of self-in-the-future is a very significant motivational tool. However, at certain times in life, such as adolescence, an individual may have no images or only negative ones. This can be a dangerous period. The individual who has no clearly defined image of him- or herself in the future, or only negative images, can at worst, be headed toward serious psychological trouble. At best, the child with no images, or only negative images, can be making choices based on fate and chance. With no future images and resultant plans and goals, behavior is oriented toward the "now" with no inclination or orientation toward future-time. If an individual's image of the future is negative there is little to motivate and little to strive for. When an individual examines future possibilities and how those possibilities may be shaped by him or her, he or she takes a major step toward establishing and working for a future goal.

Living in the future is that time-orientation which is based on anticipation. Most individuals construct mental images of the future, plan, and prepare, whether it is for next summer's vacation or a distant retirement. Throughout our lives we develop images of future possibilities and our future-selves.

Some images come from concentrated efforts at visualization, others from the media, and still others "bubble up" from the sub- and conscious self with no prompting. These mental images guide us and eventually become a major determinant of our actions and behavior in the present. "An even more powerful motivational force is a person's vision or image of himself or herself in the future — expectations of what persons will become relative to what they are in the present are considered powerful determinants of behavior. (Torrance, 1979b; Torrance & Hall, 1980)

Images change as we mature. Some are out-grown while others are discarded after we suceed in making the image part of our reality. "Images direct our actions and drive our dreams of what could be. They clarify our values and pave the way to more preferable choices. In short, 'guiding images' are bridges or roadmaps that help us move from where we are, to where we want to be. (Whaley, 1984)

Do Linkages Exist Between Time Orientation, Motivation, and Performance? Linking student time orientation, motivation, and performance is an area which suffers from lack of research. However, one can look at available information and speculate about the causal linkages involved. Available information in this case focuses on the results of the 1991 SAT scores and related demographics of those who took the test. The intent here is to contrast the student performance of those students oriented toward living in the future and performance of other students who dwell primarily in one of the two other temporal dimensions.

The recent release of the 1991 SAT Test Score information was accompanied by the disappointing news from the College Board that the average 1991 score fell to its lowest since 1983. It would appear that the percentage of students who scored high has stayed reasonably consistent over the past decade; however, the low scorers are scoring even lower. Regardless of the debate over the SAT in certain areas, what concerns us here is the correlation of scores to certain demographics.

With a national average score of 896 the College Board statisticians set about analyzing a number of demographics, several of which are related to socio-economic status. Three interesting S.E.S./performance combinations were noted:

> (1) Family income: The average score was 997 for students whose family income
> is over $70,000. This figure dropped steadily to 768 for students whose family
> income is under $10,000.

(2) Education level of the parents: Another correlation existed between the educational level of parent(s) and their child's SAT score. The scores of students whose parent(s) were not high school graduates averaged 748, while those whose parent(s) had a bachelors degree averaged 939. Those whose parent(s) had earned a graduate degree averaged 1004.

(3) Computer literacy: One last demographic oriented toward a S.E.S. breakdown should be cited: computer literate students averaged 944, while those with no computer experience averaged 862.

Level of parent education, family income level, computer literacy, all of which are directly related to socio-economic status, yield an interesting picture. Based on the above demographics, it would appear there is a connection between: (a) those having higher SAT scores, higher levels of S.E.S., and a future time orientation, and, (b) those having lower SAT scores, a lower S.E.S., and a time orientation toward the past or the present.

Why is there a connection between S.E.S. and a person's time orientation? Perhaps this quote will lend a better understanding: "The predominant American middle-class orientation is toward the future." There is good evidence that the middle class in American society, influenced by the Protestant Ethic, have typically passed on to their children a time perspective that discounts the present and looks forward to the future. This concern with the future, when transformed into personal terms holds the ingredients for success in a culture geared to future rather than the past. (Singer, 1974)

Guiding Images, The Anticipated Self, and The Disadvantaged Child

An individual's self-image projected into the future becomes the future-focused-role-image, also known as the "anticipated self." This projected self-image can literally dictate an individuals behavior in the present. How far our "anticipated-selves" are from current reality determines the degree of motivation and behavior pattern(s) we take to incorporate the images into our reality. If our actions are appropriate and successful, we realize our goal and set about developing new short and long term images of ourselves. Psychologist Erik Erickson has stated that the child tries to comprehend possible future roles, or, at any rate, to understand what roles are worth imagining... his learning... leads away from his own limitations and into future possibilities. Through imaging, the child attempt to anticipate what his life would be like if he were in different roles in the future — this process then generates the "anticipated-selves" which may or may not become a part of reality, depending on the childs motivation levels.

When children hold a strong, positive, future image of themselves they are drawn to it by ordering their actions and behavior in such a way as to realize the image of that "anticipated-self." Positive future expectations and images motivate us toward realizing those expectations. "Futurists are strong advocates of such imaging by individuals. They believe that persons' images of themselves in the future can only lead them to strive for its actualization." (Khatena, 1982) One example of the motivational and behavioral influence of future images is the image of self as a holder of a college degree. As a result of this image, one shapes his or her behavior in such a way to someday walk across the stage and be handed a diploma. Many activities and behaviors which would diminish or deny the realization of our college graduate image are postphoned. We know becoming a college graduate will help us in the future.

Knowing the results of working now for a future reward is not only a significant motivational force; but as in the above case of college graduate, it also became a primary behavior determinant. We all know of others whose image was not as strong, or perhaps had a living in the present orientation. A living in the present time orientation and working toward an image of "anticipated-self" as college graduate (the result of a living in the future time orientation) are incompatable. They cannot co-exist. Either one time orientation has to go or the individual has to exercise some self-discipline behavior. Whether or not the person walked the stage and received a diploma tells you what ultimate choice was made.

The Importance of Mental Images of the Future

Benjamin Singer, as edited by Alvin Toffler (1974), once wrote: "The future-focused role-image is our self-image projected into the future, and it lends meaning to much of what we do in the present." We anticipate different selves at different times in the future and act to realize or minimize the results of becoming those imaged future-selves. When an individual, society, or civilization has no positive image(s) to work for, the future looks bleak and unworthy of effort. The need for image building, especially with regard to the future, is undeniable. Individuals as well as whole societies thrive on guiding images and falter when there are none.

The famous Dutch futurist, Fred Polak, worked with the influence of guiding images on cultures, societies, and even civilizations. One of his final conclusions was: "Our time is the first in the memory of man which has produced no images of the future, or only negative ones." (Polak, 1973)

Whereas Polak's statement might be considered exaggeration by some, it is not without truth. "Each of us, throughout our lives, develop images of the future. Some are quite personal; some are shared by a great many others. An example of a personal image is a career goal of helping to solve problems of major urban areas. An example of a more widely held guiding image would be to eliminate starvation on this planet by the year 2000. Our orientation toward the future is based on making these mental images become a part of our reality. Several of our current and future actions are based on the probabilities of these images actually occurring. Some are positive and desirable, others are negative and undesirable. Many of our actions are aimed at achieving those images which are desirable and avoiding those images which are harmful. If the image is powerful enough, a great deal of time could be spent in its pursuit or avoidance." (Whaley, 1986)

Often, much of our time is oriented toward: 1) imaging certain possibilities, and 2) planning appropriate measures either to increase or to decrease the probability of the imaged possibilities occurrences. It doesn't matter whether we are considering a shopping trip or planning a long-range budget. We can lead better lives, both qualitatively and quantitatively, by looking ahead.

Many factors influence our images of the future. Parents, friends, books, movies, the media, and other stimuli interact to form our images of the future. These same sources combine to give us images of the past before our memory. Frequently, our images are a combination of our perceptions of past occurrences, current situations, and possible future trends. These perceptions, based on specific knowledge or intuitive feelings, frequently form the bases of our guiding images, which in turn establish our goals and influence our behavior.

Whether our mental images are based on specific knowledge or intuition, they greatly influence our actions, attitudes, life goals and values. Some guiding images are shared by a number of people. If enough people share a guiding image, the possibility of realizing the guiding image becomes very significant. The type of change which results from a large number of people sharing an image is very powerful. One example would be the sharing and resultant spread of the concept of freedom throughout Eastern Europe and the Soviet Union.

The ease and success with which we move into the future, especially during times of rapid change, has a lot to do with how well we plan and work toward achieving our guiding images. Time, the organism which could best adapt increased its chances of survival. In addition to becoming more adaptable, being able to conceptualize a future—and the foresight that emerges from that process—allows the species to become a part of that future.

The Discrepant Future of Youth

In 1986-87 more than 600,000 students in grade 2 through junior high participated in a national survey of perspectives and attitudes on the future. In the very revealing results of this study, "a majority of these students foresee a grim U.S. and international future but also, paradoxically, a promising personal future." (*The Futurist*, 1987). This discrepancy in a student's perception of a bright personal future and, at the same time, a bleak outlook on global futures, is not atypical. It is dangerous though. In this situation, the student is saying: 1) I don't have a good understanding of the interdependence of the future, 2) I don't see myself as a contributing member in the "global village"/ I'm not empowered to affect change, 3) the happenings of the world, good or bad, will not affect my life and, 4) I don't have a good guiding image of the future which is grounded in reality.

In an effort to understand better how and why this discrepancy exists in most students, a classroom teacher can initiate several exploratory discussions, writing exercises, skits, and readings. By using these strategies teachers and parents can help students explore: 1) images of the future and, 2) images of themselves in the future. In terms of overall motivation and performance, it is important to know what your students' images are, and thus, what their orientations to the future really are. For example, through a scenario writing exercise the teacher may find that many students' perception of their personal and global futures are mutually exclusive, with no connections being made. On the other hand, a teacher may find that this year's particular class maintains good motivation levels and are naturally curious about the future, whether personal or more global.

The scenario writing process is adaptable to all ages and offers the type of perspective and attitude-building helpful in creating a better future. This type of creative writing allows the inclusion of both realism and imagination, both comprehensiveness and uncertainty of plot, and perhaps most important, scenarios allow students to examine their values and attitudes about the future as they think about future possibilities and what would happen if those possibilities became reality. Teaching children to establish positive, clearly defined, sophisticated, yet flexible and realistic future images of themselves is perhaps one of the best coping skills we may impart. Start by asking: "What image(s) do I hold of myself in the future? How am I progressing toward realizing the image(s)? What type of behavior should I exhibit to realize the image(s)? In what ways might I construct guiding images which are both personal and also more global in nature? By developing new or refining old images of self-in-the-future we promote flexible thinking and flexible attitudes toward the future. The use of guiding images is like a cycle: The individual forms future-focused images which lead to certain behaviors and actions, which lead to successfully realizing the goal (either becoming or avoiding the initial image). Then new images are generated setting the whole process in motion again. This cycle happens over and over in most all our lives.

Image —> Behavior —> Goal(s) —> Image —>Behavior —> Goal(s) —> Etc.

We know from behavioral psychology that behavior successfully reinforced is behavior which is very likely to be repeated. Success breeds success, and when it comes to shaping one's future, students can learn how to make the future happen instead of being relegated to a spectator role, letting others create their future for them.

The development of healthy attitudes about oneself and the future is becoming more and more important. In the light of the seeming discrepancy in many students images of the future, a well-balanced futures studies experience "should ultimately begin to force confrontations between discrepant images. The task of helping young people make logical connections between events and consequences, with the

9

objective of developing a vision of the future that is at least coherent, if not a seamless whole, may be the most important task for educators..." (*The Futurist*, 1987) The classroom is a perfect setting for open-ended discussions of future possibilities. Teachers should strive to build the futures awareness first, the healthy attitudes will follow. In this approach a teacher's primary task would be to show children the future as a glass half full, not half empty.

Sometimes, our ability to determine the right action and behavior depend upon our perceptions of ourselves, our world, and developments that will impact on both. Such perceptions call for a more global and holistic point of view.

Macro or Global Futures

When younger children are asked how they see themselves as adults, they often come up with a fairly optimistic scenario which is usually materialistic. Life will treat them well and, more than likely, they expect to be about the same or better off than their parents. In addition, their view of the future is not much different from today, showing that exploration of possibilities and alternatives has not been given much thought.

On the other hand, when the same children are asked about the world and its overall condition, they often indicate pessimistic and negative perspectives—warfare, starvation, technological disasters. This situation is compounded if the child is identified for gifted programming. The question emerges: "How can so many children have a bright and optimistic perception of their personal future and simultaneously perceive our mutual global futures with such a bleak outlook?" Research (Torrance, 1977; Gallagher and George, 1978) shows that gifted learners often exhibit a more pessimistic attitude toward the future, yet are more capable of generating solution-oriented (vs. problem-oriented) responses than their chronological peers. The ability to generate solution-oriented responses is, and will continue to be, a highly prized ability for coping with change. However, the societal ramifications of children growing up in fear of the future, or having a fragmented and unrealisitic view of the future are significant.

CHARACTERISTICS OF FORESIGHT
Developing The Characteristics of Foresight

The following characteristics may be developed in the classroom. Familiarizing yourself with these characteristics will also help you identify programs and materials oriented toward developing skills necessary for better futures. Children developing these characteristics will be better prepared to make decisions about their personal, and our mutual, futures. Characteristics of Foresight include:

1) A talented observer who is sensitive to changes in his or her environs.

The development of this characteristic leads to identifying and understanding the major trends and issues shaping our future.

2) A capable problem solver, who can piece together seemingly unrelated events/situations and can recognize complex patterns.

Mastery of problem-solving calls for the development of higher order thinking skills, a conceptual understanding of systems, and a more holistic point of view.

3) A good data collector familiar with many types of information bases and their delivery systems.

Tools which help us create, store, manipulate, and disseminate information will continue to drive our information age for some time to come. Familiarity with such systems allow us to keep abreast of current information and knowledge, a must in the information age.

4) A flexible and caring individual, who understands the nature of change and can develop sophisticated and positive ways of thinking about, coping with, and contributing to the future.

Change is projected as a long-range constant. It can be exhilarating, challenging and seen as a promise of good things to come, or it can be misunderstood and debilitating. Flexible thinking and the ability to create options are two of the best coping skills we can give to children.

THE GOALS AND OBJECTIVES OF FUTURES STUDIES

As with any area of study, goals and objectives must be stated to guide us in developing challenging activities and an appropriate educational experience for the student. The goals of futures studies stated below have been modified and adapted from Draper Kauffman's 1976 NEA publication: *Futurism and Future Studies.*

THE GOALS OF FUTURES STUDIES

There are four primary goals of the study of alternative futures adapted for the classroom. These goals are measurable, although some more than others. All are extremely desirable for students who will live out their lives in a rapidly changing and challenging future. The individual implementing futures must ask the often confounding, curriculum question: "Are these specific goals for demonstrated mastery OR, are these simply desirable goals to be taught to?" This question will have to be answered by those implementing the futures perspective. The answer will depend almost soley upon their specific needs and intent.

Of these four goals, two are oriented toward developing skills, one goal is oriented toward development of attitudes, and one is a combination of both skill and attitude development. The "supporting objectives," enumerated in parenthesis after each goal, indicate which objectives are directly tied to the achievement of each goal. Each activity in the Activity Section (Section VI) promotes these various goals and objectives. Additionally, the beginning of each activity indicates the specific Goal(s) and Characteristic(s) of Foresight directly involved in the activity.

The I.F. Model presented in Sections I-IV, as with any model, must be based upon goals. The format which follows is presented to help you when designing activities beyond those in this book. The following goals lead the way toward the development of a futures-focused student:

(1) Development of thinking skills and a conceptual framework necessary to understand complex systems. (supporting objectives: 2, 3, 4, 6, 9, 10)

(2) Development of abilities to identify and understand major trends and issues which will shape the future. (supporting objectives: 2, 4, 5, 6, 9, 10)

(3) Development of more sophisticated and positive ways of thinking about alternative future possibilities. (supporting objectives: 7, 8, 9, 10)

(4) Development of an understanding of the nature of change and a means for coping with rapid change. (supporting objectives: all)

The achievement of these goals allows the learner to master important processes, including flexibility of thinking and attitudes which will prove priceless throughout life.

THE OBJECTIVES OF FUTURES STUDIES

As with the goals stated above, the objectives of futures studies are divided into categories of skill development, attitudinal development, or a combination. This simple labeling is done to help simplify any evaluation process. By earmarking a goal or objective as intending to foster the development of a skill or an attitude, designing evaluation criteria may be simplified.

The first six objectives focus on the development of specific skills. The seventh objective deals with the development of attitudes and perspectives as they relate to future situations. The remaining objectives focus on various combinations of skill and attitudinal development.

The objectives of futures studies are designed so the student may:

(1) Develop skills oriented toward generating preferable futures for maximum stakeholders. (SKILL)

(2) Develop ability to recognize possibilities and generate numerous alternatives and options. (SKILL)

(3) Develop skills leading to *solution-oriented* versus *problem-oriented* responses. (SKILL)

(4) Research and integrate information from a variety of diverse sources, conventional and electronic. (SKILL)

(5) Understand and utilize various forecasting methodologies. (SKILL)

(6) Develop SKILLS of value to a "citizen of the future":
   * Open-ended, divergent thinking
   * Flexibility and originality of thought
   * Exploration of causality and linkages
   * Creative problem-solving skills
   * Planning and decision making skills
   * Communication skills

(7) Develop ATTITUDES of value to a "citizen of the future":
   * Risk taking versus risk aversion
   * Concern for various stakeholders
   * Inclination for generating preferable futures
   * Perceive self as a contributing member in the "global village"
   * Perceive self as pro-active with respect to creating own future
   * Clarify personal values on issues of the future

(8) Develop ability to establish meaningful short and long-term goals. (SKILL & ATTITUDINAL)

(9) Recognize forces and trends shaping our personal and mutual futures. (SKILL & ATTITUDINAL)

(10) Recognize impacts of accelerated change on our lives and discover ways of coping with rapid change. (SKILL & ATTITUDINAL)

These goals and objectives can be used to modify existing curriculum to include: (1) specific courses in futures studies, or (2) the development of a futures theme in previously implemented course offerings. Either way, they represent worthwhile outcomes for students who will spend much of their lives in a society and world filled with challenges and opportunities, and in which change will continue to be a primary driver.

13

THE TEN GENERIC CONCEPTS, THE NINE GENERIC ISSUES, AND USING ISSUE-BASED CURRICULUM

Higher order thinking skills, creativity, and creative approaches to problem-solving are three of the primary outcomes of futures studies. Each of these are process oriented as opposed to content oriented. The need for a balance between factual information and a more process-oriented approach is best illustrated by a quote from Toffler's twenty-two year old classic, *Future Shock*:

> "Given further acceleration, we can conclude that knowledge will grow increasingly perishable. Today's 'fact' becomes tomorrow's 'misinformation'. This is no argument against learning facts or data, far from it. But a society in which the individual constantly changes his job, his place of residence, his social ties and so forth, places an enormous premium on learning efficiency. Tomorrow's schools must therefore teach not merely data, but ways to manipulate it. Students must learn how to discard old ideas, how and when to replace them. They must, in short, learn how to learn." (Toffler, 1970)

When students understand an issue from a conceptual point of view, they are thinking at a higher level and have started establishing a conceptual framework into which information may be sorted. This part of Section II shows how students can relate a concept to an issue influencing the future.

The following ten generic concepts were chosen because of the broad extent of their meanings and applicability to past/present/futuristic concerns on personal and global levels. The ten concepts are some of the most commonly illustrated in our lives. They are called generic because they are not time specific and have both personal and global meanings and applications. Because they are generic does not mean that they are simplistic in operation. For example, the nature of systems and interdependence in our world is extremely complex, requiring higher level skills to examine and better understand the nature and degree of complexity.

CONCEPT / DEFINITION:

SYSTEMS: A set of components working together to perform a function.

INTERDEPENDENCE: Mutually dependent or relying on each other.

CHANGE: Passage from one place, state, or form to another.

CONFLICT: To be in opposition, at variance; controversy through differing interests.

COMMUNICATION: The conveyance or interchange of thoughts, opinions, or information by speech, writings, signs or signals.

CULTURE: Sum total of ways of living built by a people and transmitted from generation to generation.

POPULATION: The aggregate of organisms living in a region under consideration.

HUMAN DIGNITY: The inherent worth of an individual.

TECHNOLOGY: The bridge between knowledge and practical use of materials and resources.

ENVIRONMENT: The total of surrounding conditions or influence.

Together, these ten generic concepts form a conceptual framework which aids the learner in moving from the specifics of an issue or situation, to the larger picture. A major advantage of mastering this conceptual framework is directly related to the changing nature of information and knowledge. In our world, the myriad issues, situations, and events change daily. However, the meaning of the concepts which underpin and shed more light on these daily occurrences, stays the same. That is the advantage of a concept over incidental or factual information.

For example, the *nature* of conflict will remain the same whether it is represented by a sibling rivalry, a debate between students, a football game, labor-management negotiations, an oppressive government and the people—the illustrations are endless. Because examples of situations which illustrate a concept are endless, the student can more easily see linkages between events and issues, making the principles, or underpinnings, of the concept more transferable to various situations within the child's life.

The ten generic concepts provide a framework of lasting importance. The information deluge, resultant knowledge found, and change set in motion are all inextricably linked. The conceptual framework allows students to "sort" the information into a meaningful and higher order conceptual understanding. Information is comprised of issues, situations, and events which change constantly. Concepts stay the same and thus, more closely approximate knowledge.

This is not to say that factual information should be disregarded. What this section is suggesting is that education finds more of a balance between giving factual information and working with concepts in the classroom. This would be a more appropriate approach given the forces and trends at work in our society which are changing our understanding of what knowledge is.

THE NINE ISSUES INFLUENCING THE FUTURE

Just as there are concepts which are generic in nature, there are also issues which have widespread application. A reason for this widespread applicability is that just as with the Ten Generic Concepts, the principles underpinning these specific issues are not time-specific. Humankind has been struggling with some of these issues for centuries. Other issues are much newer to our civilization; a result of more people, more information, more technology, and concomitant problems springing from combinations of these three factors. As the rate of societal change and size of our global population increases, so does a need for re-examination and resolution of the problems.

In any newspaper, on any day, one can find dozens of situations illustrating these issues. The ways in which these issues are manifested may be different from one time to another, but *the issue driving the problems remain the same.* The Nine Generic Issues coupled with the Ten Generic Concepts provide an open-ended framework for exploring the hows and whys of many of the forces actively shaping our mutual futures, their ramifications upon us, and possible resolutions.

THE NINE GENERIC ISSUES
ISSUE TITLE / CONCOMITANT QUESTION(S):

The Values Issue: What will/do we believe in?

The Quality/Quantity Issue: Is more better? What is "the good life"?

The Equity Issue: What is FAIR, not just EQUAL?

The Power/Credibility Issue: Who shall hold power and to what end(s)? Will the arrangement be perceived as credible and workable to the majority?

The Institutional Crisis Issue: Can institutions formed in one epoch for specific purposes, function appropriately in other circumstances?

The Loss of Guiding Image/Lack of Future-Focused Role Image Issue: Do we have consensus on our Nation's future directions. Do our youngsters have positive, or any, image of "self-in-the-future"?

The Domination Ethic Issue: Will the human drives to dominate destroy us? (Domination of other nations; the environment, etc.)

The Have vs. Have Not Issue: Is this the Pandora's Box of the future?

The Widening Knowledge Gap Issue: Could emerging differences between information producers and "the man on the street" eventually feed an Orwellian technocracy?

*Several issue titles are adopted from a curriculum seminar of Dr. Harold Shane, Indiana University, 1976. The Nine Generic Issues, coupled with the conceptual framework, may provide a look into many forces which are actively shaping our mutual futures. Coupling these Nine Generic Issues with the Ten Generic Concepts provides an open-ended framework for exploring the how and why of major issues and their possible resolutions. The ways in which these issues are manifested will differ from time to time, but just as with the conceptual framework, the nature or meaning of the issue driving the problem(s) will remain the same.

USING AN ISSUE-BASED CURRICULUM

The goal of an Issue-Based Curriculum (IBC) is to: (a) engage the learner in open-ended activities involving, (b) interdisciplinary material, which examines (c) themes, topics, issues, situations, and concepts in order to (d) enhance original and flexible thinking of relative complexity or sophistication. In short, IBC offers learners opportunities to examine, think about, and be a part of, life around them.

Because IBC focuses on "real-life" issues:

(1) there are no predetermined, absolute, correct answers,

(2) there is opportunity for flexible thinking, values clarification, and attitude development,

(3) the newspaper may serve as a supplemental "textbook" in most, if not all, content areas,

(4) there is ample opportunity for role-playing and use of simulations in the classroom.

Analyzing and Studying Issues

Using a conceptual framework when analyzing issues can be a great aid to the learner. Again, the primary reason is that issues, events, and situations change daily while concepts remain the same. The concept of "systems" will stay the same whether it describes a simple thermostat, the electrical system of an automobile, an interstate transportation system, or our global weather systems.

These four steps will help students better analyze and understand issues:

(1) Use the conceptual framework (the Ten Generic Concepts & Nine Generic Issues) to identify and define the issue. I.e. identify which concepts and generic issues are operating: a) directly and, b) indirectly in this issue.

(2) Gather the viewpoints of others on the issue; identify who the stakeholders are and define their interests. (i.e. What are their involvements? i.e. Why is this an issue to them? What are the different points of view? Why is there more than one point of view?)

(3) Consider the societal, environmental, technological, global equity/human rights impacts and implications of various outcomes of the issue. (I.e. if this occurred, what would be the results? The Futures Wheel described in Section IV would be a good tool to aid the student in this step.)

(4) Develop a personal viewpoint with supporting rationale.

The use of the newspaper to illustrate these issues and concepts in the real world is invaluable. Even the smallest newspaper will yield dozens of examples of the Ten Concepts and Nine Issues in action. Identifying issues in the newspaper and using an issue-based approach is highly recommended for several reasons. As a supplemental activity, examining issues through news analysis allows students to: (1) identify local or more global trends and issues which may be shaping their personal and global futures, (2) experience thinking in conceptual terms, (3) through inductive reasoning, move from specific news facts and information to the issue's/story's conceptual underpinning(s), and (4) sharpen reading and analytical skills, and (5) work with real-life issues.

CREATING AN INTERDISCIPLINARY PERSPECTIVE

The study of alternative futures calls for a curriculum design which reveals and stresses the interdependence, coherence, causal relationships, and general wholeness of our actions on future prospects. Divisions of knowledge and information based exclusively upon disciplines tends to compartmentalize, fragment, and lead us to a discontinuous and static view of situations. The traditional, reductionist approach fails to alert us adequately to the forces affecting our lives and our ability to affect future possibilites. Categorizing information by disciplines has its strengths and will continue to have educational value—especially in those fields where specialization is necessary, such as neurology, and corporate tax law. However, a more appropriate balance between disciplinary and interdisciplinary approaches in today's public education curriculum is needed. As mentioned before, our conventional way of cataloging information by disciplines will always have a place, but is increasingly inadequate as the *only* cataloging format or representation of information. Knowledge, in all fields, is growing exponentially. A balance in the approach used to describe knowledge and information is becoming increasingly necessary.

There is no single discipline to which the study of alternative futures belongs; there is a futuristic application or aspect to every discipline. The art of speculation and conjecture about future possibilities must be open-ended. In this type of learning, the primary role of the instructor is that of a facilitator of resources and research skills.

The use of an interdisciplinary perspective in futures studies gives students a more holistic picture of: 1) what they are learning and its connection to other information and, 2) how it relates to their world and future. The "truth" to interdisciplinary approaches lies in the fact that with increasing research and subsequent information flow, we find concepts and data from one subject are increasingly applicable to other areas. Examples may be found in combinations of new and old information from new areas such as astrophysics and bio-technology. These "disciplines" are interdisciplinary, drawing on information from a number of diverse areas. The interdisciplinary perspective frees the teacher and students from the constaints of information limited to one content area. Instead, the student may use a more open-ended pursuit of information by proceeding along a path of information acquisition in and out of specific disciplines. As a by-product, the student sees interconnections not necessarily apparent when viewed soley from a single content area.

The traditional, content area approach gives students indepth information in one narrow and, because of the way we usually have to teach it, isolated area. Due to this approach, a reduction in a holistic viewpoint occurs. This is exactly the opposite of what is needed by students during a point in their lives when they are struggling to put together an accurate view of the world and their place in it. A steady diet of specific disciplinary content, without a balancing interdisciplinary perspective on information and knowledge, will lead to knowing a great deal about a narrow content focus. Synthesizing information into a holistic or "generalist" point of view becomes very difficult. Perhaps the synthesis may never happen at the level needed by the student to understand better current and future developments.

The nature of our world is incredibly complex. Our lives and our futures are interconnected—we live in an interdisciplinary design. This fact was always there, but it is becoming more difficult to avoid. During the information age it appears the more we learn, the more we are forced to realize the interrelatedness of natural and man-made systems, cosmic and sub-atomic. Alfred North Whitehead observed: "New epochs emerge with comparative suddenness." Little of the industrial age, with its factories and smokestacks, has anything to do with preparing students for a future in the Information

Age, represented by computers and satellites. The Information Age will eventually change the way we educate people. It will take time, but this is more a problem of changing an educational instututiton remarkably resistant to change, than it is indicative of the need for change.

DEVELOPING A FUTURES PERSPECTIVE ACROSS DISCIPLINES

The need for an interdisciplinary perspective within futures material grows from three sources:

    1) The nature of the conceptual framework and an issue-based approach,

    2) The nature of information age learning, and

    3) The nature of our world.

The nature of the conceptual framework and an issue-based approach is such that student research on any of the generic issues and concepts, singularly or in combination, often requires gathering information across many disciplines. An example of an advanced futures research question is: "From what sources may I gather information on the interdependence of population growth, pollution levels, and food production?"

This question will lead the student researcher across many different disciplines. For example:

— In **mathematics**: the nature of exponential growth, ratios (mortality to birth rates) statistical information on population(s).

— In **social studies**: government demographic information, the nature of psychological crowding, the "have vs have nots" issue.

— In **science:** the types, composition, and impact of pollutants, the nature of any population (i.e. it continues to expand), chemical vs. organic farming.

— In **literature/reading**: fiction and non-fiction dealing with the future and those issues and challenges likely to be found there: *Soyent Green, Brave New World, The Limits to Growth, Looking Backward, Dune, Stranger in a Strange Land,* etc.

— In **creative writing**: developing scenarios focusing on solutions to our population/pollution problems.

— In **independent study:** developing projects of all types focusing on some aspect of the future.

In pursuit of this question the student will not only find information relevant to the question but also see the interconnectedness of the information across content areas. At this point the teacher's task of promoting work which leads to the student transfering that information becomes much easier.

For an interdisciplinary activity to use in your classroom see Activities 25 & 26 in the Activities Section (Section VI).

19

STEPS FOR DEVELOPING AN INTERDISCIPLINARY CURRICULUM UNIT

Before beginning any specific steps the teacher must choose a topic or thematic area which: 1) compliments the regular course of study, 2) is neither too broad nor too narrow to allow meaningful exploration, and 3) is relevant and interesting to students and has applicability across disciplines.

1) Establish goals, a general outline, and a timeline for the topical/thematic unit.

2) Develop the criteria for evaluation of student outcomes during and after the unit.

3) Check availability of resources needed to run and/or enhance the unit.

4) Establish performance objectives based on the goals in #1.

5) Design the activities needed to reach objectives.

6a) Determine *commonalities* between content areas involved in interdisciplinary unit.

6b) Establish *"catalyst questions"* based on the commonalities, which are broad and require the student to bring together information from past experiences in the different content areas. In the Humanities, for example: Why does Humankind create? Why does Humankind attempt utopias?

Commonalities : common themes or issues which run through different content areas.

Catalysts questions : broad-based questions which are conceptual in nature and call for the student to focus on commonalities between content areas.

---

7) Revise #3 and #5 as needed now that the commonalities and catalyst questions are established.

8) Implement the unit, evaluate the results, and modify as needed.

NOTE: C. June Maker in her book: *Curriculum Development for the Gifted Child* (1982) outlines a process for setting up a "cross-discipline seminar" using Hilda Taba's approaches (p. 337-343).

USING THE "INTERDISCIPLINARY WHEEL"

Futures studies is a topical and thematic area which has application across all content areas. The interdisciplinary wheel is a tool which allows us to see, and make use of, those interconnections. The interdisciplinary wheel is a simple planning device for the teacher to "web" or chart the different applications of specific information to a larger content area. It is a simple "futures wheel" which is modified for a lesson planning use. The use of a "futures wheel" (described in Section IV: Futures Research Tools and Methodologies) allows a specific theme, topic, issue, event, or situation to be placed in a context for use with students as they move from one content area to another. The topic, etc. is then examined to determine which concepts are driving its emergence and development.

EXAMPLE:

1) Pick a topic from the "40 Future Topics" listed in the Independent Study Section i.e., "Weather Modification: Good or Bad?"

2) Next, determine the primary concepts driving the topic by using the Ten Generic Concepts listed in Section II. The generic concepts **directly** involved in a weather modification study would include: Environment, Change, Sytems/Interdependence, and Technology.

3) Using the Interdisciplinary Wheel, place the topic to be examined in the middle and web the various implications and catalyst questions for different content areas.

Economics
How could weather modification improve global harvests? What countries could benefit the most economically?

Language Arts
Create a scenario based on: What changes in your life would occur as a result of weather modification?

Math
What are the average mean temps. & rain for selected sites?

Weather Modification

Science/English
Interview meterologists for information on the processes involved in trying to modify the weather also the difficulties, effects, benefits, etc. Put this information into a report to share in class.

Geography
What parts of the world's climate could benefit from weather modification? Explain why you made your choices.

Below is a series of extended catalyst questions for exploration which could arise from the topic of weather modification.

In **science**: What type of technology would it take to manipulate such a large system? What scientific fields would be involved, Physics? Biology? Meterology? a new combination?) Once the change started could it be controlled? (nature of systems/physics) What would/could happen to the Earth's surface and oceans if weather control was achieved? (geology, oceanography, etc.) Is there reason to believe that shifts in weather have occurred in various parts of the world in the past? (archaeology, possibly anthropology, geology)

In **mathematics**: How could Humankind change its population growth, distribution, birth and mortality rates? (exponential growth, demographics)

In the **social studies**: How could weather modification change the economic outlook of the entire world? In terms of need, which two geographic areas of the world should become a priority for immediate application of weather modification technology.

In **English** (Composition/creative writing): Write a scenario in which: 1) weather modification is achieved and is successful in bringing economic well-being to the world population, and 2) global and/or regional weather modification becomes a "product" controlled by a few technocrats and available to the highest bidder.

FUTURES RESEARCH TOOLS AND METHODOLOGIES

A proven set of research tools are indispensible to anyone who wants to explore future possibilities and create options for those possibilities. Exploring different future possibilities such as space or undersea colonization can be exciting in itself since one "purpose of the study of possible futures is to anticipate the consequences of current trends." (Gallagher, 1985) However, looking at the ramifications of those current trends and their meanings to us personally and globally requires certain methodologies for better understanding. Although it is difficult to know exactly what "the future" will hold for us, it is possible to reach an understanding of some highly probable events and their impact. "It is commonplace among those engaged in futures research to note that their subject matter does not exist. Once the decision is made to scrutinize the future, there is seemingly nothing to focus on. Yet futurists go ahead and study it anyway. They do this, of course, through their understanding of where current momentum and present decisions will lead. Futures studies is the effort to anticipate and prepare for the future before it unfolds." (Fowles, 1978)

All the research methodologies in this section are simplified versions of actual research tools used in the field. The basic premises and principles upon which these tools operate are the same, but most statistical processes have been left out. By using the research methodologies and thinking skills in this book, the teacher can facilitate approaches to problem-solving, techniques for information creation and retrieval, and flexibility of thinking. A majority of research tools described for the model have commonalities. All of the tools can provide baseline information for use in a scenario.

All of the following research tools:

1) require divergent and convergent production and evaluation,
2) lead to a better understanding of causal linkages/cause and effect,
3) lead to a better understanding of systems and interdependence,
4) require students to cite possibilities and options,
5) enhance higher-order thinking and problem-solving skills.

The following research tools are well adapted for classroom use, and, if well executed, may yield some surprisingly accurate forecasts. This section contains a description of each tool, its strengths and capabilities, the skills it can impart to the student, and examples of how to make use of each.

A) Futures Wheel

B) Delphi Technique

C) Cross Impact Matrix

D) Trend Analysis

E) Trend Extrapolation

F) Techology Assessment

G) Scenario Writing

If you are interested in further exploring a wide range of futures research tools see: Fowles, J., Editor; *Handbook of Futures Research*, Greenwood Press, Westport, CT. The 800+ pages of the handbook represent one of the most comprehensive look at futures methodologies avaliable today.

CREATING A FUTURES WHEEL

Futures wheels make us more aware of the cause and effect of events. Understanding causal linkage is one of the primary objectives of forecasting. An example of causal linkage could be seen in a futures wheel which indicates an increase of population would lead to more pollution, more crowding, a need for more jobs and health care services, etc. A futures wheel demonstrates **how developments in one area automatically lead to developments in other areas: cause and effect.** The following steps will help you construct your futures wheel:

(1) Draw a large circle in the middle of your sheet of paper. Write the forecast or trend you wish to examine in the circle.

INCREASED POPULATION

(2) Draw spokes from the first circle and at the end of each spoke draw another circle. Within each of these secondary circles write a forecast you believe will be a direct consequence or effect of the initial forecast.

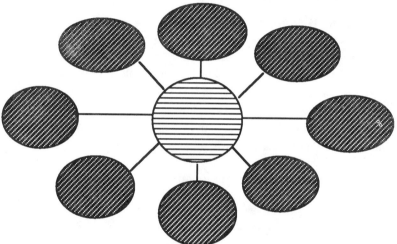

(3) Next, draw spokes from the second ring of circles and at the end of these draw other circles. Within these write a third set of forecasts which represent the effects of the second ring of forecasts.

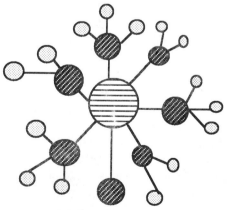

(4) Lastly, identify the circles having a common relationship to each other by coloring related circles the same color. All circles having one relationship can be red, others green, and so on.

23

THE DELPHI TECHNIQUE

The Delphi Technique gained its name from a site in ancient Greece. The wisdom of Apollo was transmitted through various mediums at this site. Many individuals came to the site seeking knowledge of the future. Because of the continuous flow of gifts to Apollo, Delphi became a rich cultural center in ancient Greece.

The Rand Corporation used the name Delphi for a technique developed in the 1950's which involved the surveying of experts to obtain an opinion based upon consensus. The methodology of the Delphi Technique is designed to get reliable answers from experts on various questions about the future. Regardless of some studies indicating the technique might not be totally reliable, it continues to be very widely used for many research projects which lead to long-range forecasts.

The anonymity of respondents is an important feature. Other than the anonymity of the respondents there are three other important features. The first is there are usually two or more rounds of questionnaires circulated to the targeted experts. The second is the respondents chosen are representative experts in the field of inquiry. The third feature is that controlled feedback to the respondents is supplied. Controlled feedback means the respondents are told the general responses of the previous round of questioning. In addition, on second or third rounds of questioning, respondents with extreme responses are asked to explain the reasoning behind their positions.

There are ten steps to the Delphi Technique:

1) Choose a team of individuals to develop and monitor the Delphi.

2) Select members of the Delphi Panel. These individuals should be experts in the area under investigation. Depending on the scale of the investigation and resources available, there should ideally be between 10 and 25 respondents. The respondents may be local, regional, national, international, or any combination. This would depend on the area of exploration, amount of time, and amount of money available for postage, etc.

3) Develop the first round of Delphi questionnaires. Typically, the first round allows more general responses which are then more specifically focused in later rounds of questioning.

4) Test the questions for appropriateness — are you asking the right questions for your area of exploration? Be sure the wording of the questions is clear and easy to answer — respondents don't generally care for questions which require essays in response.

5) Send the first round of questionnaires to the chosen panel of experts.

6) Analyze the results of the returned questionnaires.

7) Based on the analysis, prepare a second round of questions with any necessary modifications such as narrowing the focus of the questions. If there are extreme responses from the first round of questionnaires, give the panel member(s) an opportunity to explain the response.

8) Send the second round of questionnaires to the panel.

9) Analyze the returned questionnaires (steps 7 & 8 are repeated for as many rounds as you choose).

10) Prepare a report of the findings and/or conclusions.

The Delphi Technique is especially useful when analyzed event(s) lend themselves to subjective judgement instead of the more objective "number-crunching" style of technical analysis. It is also useful because the experts do not have to be brought face to face. Perhaps the most important step is number 4, insuring the clarity of the questions. If the questions are unclear and easily answered, the responses are useless.

Below is a sample of a letter containing an introduction to the project.

FRANKLIN MIDDLE SCHOOL
LONG-RANGE FORECASTING STUDY

December 10, 1992

Dear _____,

The enclosed Delphi survey is our attempt to get certain information about the future. We have been studying alternative futures recently and are very interested in your opinions as an expert in the area of _____.

We are gathering information on _____. Our survey is an attempt to get predictions regarding (1) the desirability of certain possible occurrences and (2) an approximate time frame for the occurrence.

We have established a time horizon of 50 years. It is very possible that the occurrences explored in this Delphi will have a meaningful impact upon our lives and this society. We recognize the field you are involved in is moving very quickly and is influencing the future.

Based on your expertise we are asking you to indicate your educated guesses as to when the occurrences listed below will happen. Your responses will be anonymous to the other members of our panel of experts and we will provide you with feedback from each previous round of questions. We are planning ____ rounds. We appreciate your time and expertise in helping us obtain a glimpse of the future.

Sincerely,

NOTE: As a class project, different groups of students may be put in charge of a specific task or step in the Delphi process. This cooperative effort is important to the entire operation and allows students to feel more involved in the process.

CROSS-IMPACT ANALYSIS

By setting up and analyzing a cross-impact matrix you may determine the various repercussions resulting from a specified event. The number of impacts you find are an indication of the degree of interconnectedness which exists between the variables and the event. The higher the number of impacts you find, the higher the degree of connectedness. For example, when the U.S. experiences another gasoline shortage, one potential supplemental fuel is ethanol. Suppose some farmland was switched to growing renewable sources of energy. Crops like sorghum, sugar beets, and corn yield ethanol when processed. That helps the energy problem, but what about food prices, food shortages? What if the prices of seeds, because of the rapidly building demand, caused shortages which put more strain on family-owned farms? What if this situation was compounded by one, or a series of natural disasters? "What if...?" Linkages, the course of action between cause and effect, alert us to different possibilities, both good and bad. Once possibilities are recognized and understood, alternative courses of action may be planned to minimize or avoid negative situations and attract or enhance positive situations.

In the cross-impact matrix below, four variables will be analyzed to determine their degree of interdependence. Under each variable on the vertical axis are possible directions of change: increase, decrease, etc. In the first step of analysis students would examine the influencing effects of increased population growth upon: (1) food production (2) natural resources, and (3) pollution. The results would be written on a separate sheet of paper and labeled. The results of a population increase and the effecting on food supply would be under 1a. Then the students would examine the impacts of decreased population growth upon the food supply (1b) and so on through out the entire matrix. Since it is almost impossible to analyze the impacts of one variable upon itself, these are called "empty cells." After students have identified the outcomes of one event upon the others, they should assign rough probabilities to their cross-impacts. The probabilities computed are a rough index of the interdependence between the different variables.

IF THIS EVENT OCCURS ↓	WHAT WILL BE THE IMPACTS ON THE VARIABLES BELOW?			
	POPULATION	FOOD SUPPLY & PRODUCTION	NATURAL RESOURCES	POLLUTION
POPULATION: a)INCREASES b)DECREASES c)LEVELS OFF	X	1	2	3
FOOD SUPPLY: a)INCREASES b)DECREASES c)LEVELS OFF	4	X	5	6
NAT.RESOURCE USAGE: a)INCREASES b)DECREASES c)LEVELS OFF	7	8	X	9
POLLUTION: a)INCREASES b)DECREASES c)IS CONSTANT	10	11	12	X

TREND ANALYSIS

A trend is a pattern of behavior which occurs over time. The following are four characteristics which trends frequently display:

(1) The general direction of the trend; toward growth or decline.

(2) The rate or intensity of the trend; how fast the growth or decline is happening.

(3) The general "balance" of the trend; toward steady or erratic growth/decline.

(4) The lifetime of the trend: long or short-term?

The following exercise is designed to let you explore the challenges of trending and to build your forecasting skills.

Choose a trend for analysis:_____

Analyze your trend by asking the following questions:

(1) What are the underlying causes which created the trend?

(2) Are those conditions likely to continue in the future?

(3) What new developments (i.e. new technologies) might alter the trend?

(4) Is the trend approaching some saturation point or limit?

(5) Does the trend conflict with some other trend? Which one(s)?

(6) Who does the trend benefit? (business, government etc.)

(7) Does the trend have potentially harmful consequences or side effects?

(8) Are deliberate efforts to halt the trend likely?

(9) How easily could the trend be halted?

*Questions adapted from: D. Kaufman, Futurism and Future Studies, 1976.

TREND EXTRAPOLATION

Trend extrapolation is the process of extending an analyzed trend into the future. Once the following characteristics of a trend are known, you are ready to extrapolate or project the trend into the future:

(1) The general direction of the trend; toward growth or decline.

(2) The rate or intensity of the trend; how fast the growth or decline is happening.

(3) The general "balance" of the trend; toward steady or erratic growth/decline.

(4) The lifetime of the trend: long or short-term?

COMPARING & CONTRASTING TREND ANALYSIS & TREND EXTRAPOLATION

—Trend analysis looks to the past whereas trend extrapolation projects a trend into the future.

—Trend analysis traces a trend only to the present date and no further.

—Trend analysis is a forecasting aid, trend extrapolation is a forecast.

—Extrapolating a trend into the future as a forecast is based solely on the trend's past performance. Once you've analyzed, and know the background of a trend, extrapolation is a simple, linear projection of the trend into the future.

There is a major caveat in trend extrapolation; as a forecasting tool it is only good in the short-term. Since the extrapolation of a trend is a simple linear projection into the future, it does not consider many factors or variables which could change the trend's future characteristics. In fact, the further into the future you extrapolate the trend the higher the possibility of a variable changing the trend and rendering your forecast something less than it could be.

The following exercise is designed to allow you to identify the best example of trend extrapolation based on a previously analyzed trend which has been graphed.

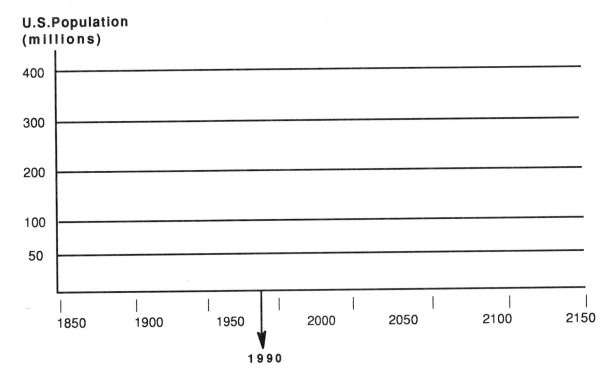

Below is data you will need to chart the population growth of the U.S. to 1990. This data would allow you to see the trend to date. After you have plotted the above information on the graph you will find that the characteristics represented in the trend on U.S. population growth are: 1) steady, 2) sustained, 3) long-term growth. After analyzing the information to date you may then examine the trend and make your best estimate of extrapolation regarding the trend's future characteristics.

Selected U.S. population figures (in millions)

1800 =	5.3
1850 =	23.2
1900 =	76.0
1940 =	132.0
1950 =	151.6
1960 =	181.0
1980 =	230.0
1985 =	236.0
1990 =	251.0

TECHNOLOGY ASSESSMENT

Technology assessment is a method of determining the effects upon society which may occur when a technology is introduced, extended, or modified. The process examines those unintended, indirect, or delayed consequences. Technology assessment allows the user to "look around the corner" and anticipate possible outcomes of certain situations in order to plan for a better, more preferable future.

The actual process used in the field is more complex than what is presented below, involving several tools including the Delphi, systems modeling, cross-impact analysis, and more. There are also statistical processes involved when used in the field. However, the essence of the process outlined below is the same and serves the purpose of requiring higher order thinking and creativity.

There are nine basic steps involved in the procedure:

1) Structuring the problem: what exactly is the problem the technology is to alleviate?

2) Determining possible impacts: if the technology is implemented as proposed, what would occur?

3) Evaluating impacts: determining the benefits and liabilities of the technology's implementation.

4) Identifying the decision makers involved: who/what agency will determine the final yes or no?

5) Identifying vested interests and ultimate goals of the decision makers.

6) Identifying possible options for the decision makers: are other possibilities available?

7) Identifying the stakeholders; the parties which have an interest: who will the technology affect — directly or indirectly, good or bad?

8) Determining conclusions, recommendations and modifications

9) Presentation of the results; written report, a "hearing," etc.

There are several opportunities to apply this process in the "Forty Future Topics" found in the Independent Study Section (Section V). There are also some specific applications of Technology Assessment to be found in the Activities Section (Section VI).

A PRIMER ON SCENARIO WRITING

A scenario is a story constructed for enhanced awareness of a particular state of affairs. A noted futurist, Herman Kahn, has defined a scenario as: "A hypothetical sequence of events constructed for the purpose of focusing attention on the cause-effect processes and decision points." Only by examining the various linkages between cause and effect can one reach a better understanding of how and why a particular situation came to exist. Past and current decisions regularly invoke unforeseen future consequences as various possibilities, or futures, are realized. Through exploring possible impacts one can better avoid the negative consequences and enhance the positive.

Scenarios are written from a future point of view looking back to the present. A scenario may be described as a "history of the future." Scenarios usually describe how a situation developed from one point to the scenario's projected future. This is done by: 1) tracing various decision points, 2) the options chosen, and 3) the cause and effect of those past decisions leading to the described future.

Scenarios should not be confused with science fiction. Science fiction: 1) is capable of a broader reach of possibilities, 2) is not necessarily tied to a particular past, and 3) is more involved in plot and character. In contrast, scenarios are a careful study of alternatives and their impact, paying particular attention to cause and effect. A scenario allows the writer to create a lengthy study of one particular future situation, the decisions leading to the situation, and all causal linkages involved.

In the classroom, scenario writing is one of the most powerful tools available to students and teachers who are thinking about the future. Creativity drives scenario writing. This type of creative writing allows the inclusion of both realism and imagination, both comprehensiveness and uncertainty of plot, and perhaps most important, scenarios allow students to examine their values and attitudes about the future as they think about future possibilities and what would happen if those possibilities became reality. Scenario writing draws upon divergent, convergent, and evaluative thinking, research and information retrieval skills, planning and forecasting skills and creative writing skills. It is an enjoyable way to allow children to think about different future situations, sharpen their thinking and writing skills, and practice creative thinking. The process is adaptable to all ages and offers the type of perspective and attitude-building helpful in creating a better future.

ELEMENTS OF SCENARIO WRITING

The structure of scenario writing is basically open-ended. Time, for example, is a major variable. The "time" could be on a near or distant horizon (i.e. 1999, or 2450). The span of time examined could be "a day in the life," or a more extensive time frame of a few decades. In a more lengthy time frame, a clear event-order and consistency are necessary so readers have an accurate picture of what-happened-when.

Another variable is the writer's point of view. Both positive and negative scenarios have merit. Negative scenarios may be written in such a way as to challenge the reader to undertake action which may help avoid the bleak forecast. On the other hand, a positive scenario brings the promise of a better quality of life, usually through various technological discoveries and concerted action by different stakeholders.

FOCUSING QUESTIONS

The development of a clearer, more focused scenario may be achieved by the writer asking certain questions. Examples of these questions might be:

(1) Are there any natural limits to the trend(s) being examined in the scenario? i.e., Finite resources: There are only so many barrels of oil.

(2) Are there artificial (man-made) limits to the trend(s) being examined? i.e., Does the proposed scenario present too radical a change over too short a time period? Would people/society reject the changes?

(3) What type of demographics are involved in the trend(s)? i.e., Will global birth/death rates interfere with the trend? Does the trend require a high school education of all people?

(4) Do specific technologies amplify or impede the trend(s)? i.e., the current trend toward increased use of nuclear energy; the current need to move people safer and faster; with current technology, could we reasonably expect to build an underwater bullet-train connecting New York with Europe in the next 5 years?

FORCING FACTORS

"Forcing factors" are events or situations of significance which have the potential to change: (1) the **direction** (up/down) of trend growth, or (2) the **rate** (fast/slow) of growth of the trend(s) being examined. Again, the consideration of these factors allows the writer to add clarification and consistency to the scenario.

Some categories of forcing factors which inhibit or amplify a trend are: 1) political events, 2) technological innovations, 3) societal changes, 4) economic shifts, and 5) ecological changes. The different effects of these five categories of forcing factors may be viewed on any number of levels. Some impact levels could be personal, local, regional, national, global, galactic, or various mixes of all.

SLIDE-TAPE PRODUCTIONS

Resources permitting, students could create a slide-tape or filmstrip production based on the written scenario. With the scenario becoming the narrative, the student(s) could collect magazine pictures which complement different aspects of the scenario. The pictures could then be made into slides and arranged in concert with the scenario's narrative. The next step would be to tape the spoken narrative to supply the audio portion of the slide-tape. A finishing touch could be to record another audio track containing only background music. Music, like photographs, can have a powerful effect on the audience's mood.

The spoken narrative and the background music could then be combined into one sound track. Placing inaudible cues at certain points will automatically forward the carousel tray of slides as your sound track plays. The finished product is an excellent way to increase the impact and response to the messages in the scenario.

For a more extensive treatment of how to make a slide-tape production from a student scenario see Activity #6 in the Activity Section.

SCENARIO FORMATS AND STARTERS

For those students who might be interested in trying their hand at scenario writing, the following "stems" and formats might be helpful. As with many written works, sometimes the most difficult part is the first few lines. There are three different scenario formats described below. Give each format a try...

A chain of events scenario:

It is the year_____. Many things have changed since the early 19__'s. The reasons these changes happened were many but the major reasons were_____. After these occurrences, and the changes they brought, people had no choice but to _____. Then with so many people changing their _____, other things began to happen. The result of all this was _____.

Example: It is the year 2020. America has reorganized itself into different regions. States have been done away with. The major reason this reorganization occurred was economics. Each region has different energy supplies which the other regions don't have. These differences made our continuing energy crisis more bearable.

Another format would be: **Looking back on history.**

The year 2020 began quietly enough. Many thought the New Year was a little like the "old days." But there were significant differences— in fact, very little was the same. The research and experimentation in the field of genetics had a lot to do with the changes. This period of research really got under way during the late 1990's. Many of the experiments dealt with creating "new" types of life. Around the turn of the century, several scientists found a way to _____.

The last major type of scenario format is known as: **A day in the life.**

I woke up to music and several people dancing on my desk. As I became more fully awake, I realized it was a "call" from some friends on my holographic *communicor*. It was my birthday— August 12, 2020. I was stationed on space colony "AQ-2," and had been involved in some terra-forming jobs; creating liveable environments on surface of the Moon.

NOTE: Another good source of scenarios for older students (i.e. Middle-High School) is: Hawken, P., Ogilvy, J., Schwartz, P. (1982). *Seven Tomorrows*. New York: Bantam Books.

INDEPENDENT STUDY

One of the essential abilities needed in the future is the ability to learn independently. Most every future employment situation imaginable will require the ability to learn independent of some external force, such as schooling. One of the primary goals of the educational system is to teach students to learn how to learn. We have all heard of the importance attached to "lifelong learning" for future professional and leisure pursuits. Independent study provides the opportunity to begin mastering life-long learning. The possibilities with independent study are many and varied. The process also easily lends itself to almost any teaching/learning situation, content area, and age of student. In today's already overloaded curriculum, content and skill-building are sometimes taught in isolation. Part of the problem is simply the time available. Another part of the problem is the lack of meaningful activities in which the student can integrate all components of the lesson. Aside from basic skill-building, independent study offers a unique opportunity to put content, such as social studies, reading/literature and science in a futures context. The types of skills sharpened by students in an independent study effort would include: question-asking, note-taking and outlining, library skills, problem-solving, creative and critical thinking. In independent study, the concepts, issues, and specific futures research tools found in other sections of this book have an opportunity to come together and help the student create original information.

The following section offers **"Forty Future Topics."** These topics include such diverse interests as: "Bio-technology: The Six Million Dollar Person Is Already Here," "Religion in the 21st Century," "Space Colonization and Industrialization," and "Wildlife Preservation and General Maintenance of Spaceship Earth." Some topics are very sophisticated and multi-faceted asking difficult questions such as: "Global Equity: The Have and the Have Not Nations." Some topics are very simple and beg more of our imagination than computers to solve. Some topics are very practical and down-to-earth such as: "Recycling Cities for People." Others are very esoteric and seemingly far-fetched for our time in history. There are topics for all ages, all grade levels. All topics will sharpen specifc skills and allow the student to become more familiar with some aspect of the future and, as a result, become more "futures-friendly."

The **"Preliminary Research Form"** found in the next part of this section is an aid for students to determine if their proposed topic is researchable or if the topic needs to be either narrowed or expanded. Sometimes it is difficult to find appropriate amounts of information on a topic because the focus is too narrow. Likewise, in our enthusiasm it is possible to bite off more than we can chew. Far from not having enough resources, there are so many we feel paralyzed— not knowing where to start. The "Preliminary Research Form" is designed to help the student target the topic and available resources.

Also, there is a suggested **"Independent Study Contract"** for teacher and student use. It is designed for use after the "Preliminary Research Form" has helped the student target the topics and resources. Other than a specific agreement between the student, teacher, and when appropriate, parent(s), it also is an important organizational tool for all involved.

The final page of Section V contains a proposed **" Research Paper Format "** for those students whose product is in the form of a written report. This format has been used successfully with students in grades 5-12. The major variables between the different grade levels are: 1) the number of pages suggested for each section of the paper, and 2) the degree of sophistication of the information. If you are working with students younger than grade five you may want to simplify it somewhat. Either way, you are invited to change it for your own specific group and/or needs.

FORTY FUTURE TOPICS

The following topics may serve as catalysts for independent study projects, research papers, or as themes in scenario writing. Although some of these topics may seem to be oriented toward supplying research topics for the upper grades, the teacher has the option of scaling down or simplifying the topic. For elementary grades, simplifying the topic may be only a matter of discussing local, more tangible, examples and illustrations in the student's known community. In other cases these topics may be explored by elementary students on a purely imaginative basis. Using only their imagination students could write about, "The World of Sports: 1999," "The Intelligence Pill," "Schools of the Future," "Farming in the Future," "The Future of Art," or any number of other topics. The list is by no means comprehensive. You are invited to add topics or "hitch-hike" on listed topics.

1. The Aging Baby Boom: Their Future Impact on American Society
2. Bio-technology: The Six Million Dollar Person Is Here
3. Where is the Family Unit Today? Where Will It Be Tomorrow?
4. Genetic Innovation (Cloning, Artificial Wombs, Embryo Transplants)
5. Current Societal Trends Which Will Shape the Future
6. Technological Growth: Good or Bad?
7. Religion in the 21st Century
8. Forecasting Tomorrow: How Is It Done?
9. Transportation: Yesterday, Today and Tomorrow
10. ESP, Body-Mind Bio-feedback, and the Potential of the Human Mind
11. Futurists: Who Are They and What Do They Do?
12. The World of Sports: 2019
13. Alternative Sources of Energy
14. The Intelligence Pill
15. Ocean Farming and Resource Extraction
16. Wildlife Preservation and General Maintenance of Spaceship Earth
17. Nuclear Waste: What Can We Do With It?
18. A Doomsday Future
19. A Utopian Future
20. Cybernetics: Make Way For The Thinking Machines
21. Our Changing Values: Today and Tomorrow
22. Schools of the Future
23. Weather Modification: Good or Bad?
24. Farming in the Future
25. The Future and Art
26. Social Roles in the Future
27. Solid Waste: Trash or Treasure?
28. Dignity in Death and Euthanasia
29. The Nature, and Impacts of, CHANGE
30. Global Equity: The Have and the Have Not Nations
31. Floating Cities and Other Macro-Engineering Projects of the Future
32. Space Colonization and Industrialization
33. What Is The "Knowledge Explosion" and "Information Society"?
34. UFO's: What If It's True?
35. Recycling Cities for People
36. Planetary and Extra-Planetary Resources for the Future
37. Robotics and the Future
38. Appropriate Technology and Voluntary Simplicity
39. Endangered Animal and Plant Species: "Once They're Gone..."
40. WATER: Do We Have A Right To Clean Water And Will There Be Enough?

FUTURES STUDIES PRELIMINARY RESEARCH FORM

Student name: _____

Proposed research project title: _____

This form will help you put together information on your proposed topic. Preliminary research is necessary to determine if you need to widen or narrow your topic. If there are very few sources available, you should consider widening your topic — if you have too many sources, you should consider narrowing it.

Encyclopedia: 1)   _____   pg# _____

                         2)   _____   pg# _____

Books: (use the card catalog under your topic)

                         1)   _____   pg# _____

                         2)   _____   pg# _____

                         3)   _____   pg# _____

Magazine Articles: (use the *Reader's Guide to Periodical Literature*)

                         1)   _____   pg# _____

                         2)   _____   pg# _____

Newspaper Articles:

                         1)   _____   pg# _____

                         2)   _____   pg# _____

Audio Visual: Films/Filmstrips/Video Recordings, etc.

                         1)   _____   Ref# _____

                         2)   _____   Ref# _____

Vertical File:

                         1)   _____   pg# _____

                         2)   _____   pg# _____

INDEPENDENT STUDY CONTRACT

Student name: _____

Project title: _____

Brief description of project: _____

Research questions:

_____
_____
_____
_____
_____

Resources will include: _____
_____

Materials will include: _____
_____

Brief description of product: _____
_____
_____

Proposed audience: _____

^^

PART II

ANY CHILD CAN BECOME GIFTED

A MANUAL FOR PARENTS & TEACHERS

INITIAL REVIEW DATE: _____ **STUDENT INITIALS:** _____

TEACHER INITIALS: _____

Date started: _____ **Date completed:** _____

Student signature: _____
_____

Teacher signature: _____
_____

Parent signature: _____

37

PROPOSED RESEARCH PAPER FORMAT
(Upper Elementary-Middle School Requirements)
Outline format for written research projects

SECTION I.   **Introduction:** What your project will focus on. Tell the reader WHY you chose your topic. Tell the reader WHY you chose the questions that you have about your topic. (1-1.5 pages)

SECTION II.   **Findings from literature:** What is being said by experts and others in magazine articles/books you have read in your search for information. This is simply a report on what already exists. (usually several citations here, 2 pages)

SECTION III.   **YOUR forecast as to what will happen:** This is a very important section. Tell the reader WHAT YOUR EDUCATED GUESS IS based on your readings/class discussions/etc. Make obvious use of the tools/methodologies (such as futures wheels, etc.) we have discussed. (3 pages)

SECTION IV.   **Bibliography:** This is where you cite the books & articles you have refered to in the paper. You will receive a handout with the citation format which the teacher has chosen for you to follow. Examples will also be given in class.

RESEARCH PAPER IN BRIEF:

Section I = Introduction: (a) What you're focusing on, (b) what questions do you want to answer, and (c)why those particular questions? In other words, tell the readers what you are going to tell them.

Section II = Findings: Tell the reader what have you found in your readings.

Section III = Forecast: This is where you finally get to tell the reader what **your** projections are based on your findings and own thinking.

Section VI = Bibliography: A bibliography will be included at the end of the paper. Share with the read the sources of information you used in the paper.

THIRTY CLASSROOM ACTIVITIES

The Activities Section is intended to give the classroom teacher immediate access to thirty useful, pertinent activities which stretch the student's mind. By challenging the student with open-ended questions and situations the student is required to use higher level thinking skills and experiences a real demand for creative thinking and problem-solving.

The activities specify for which grade level each activity is appropriate, although most activities may be modified for various grade levels. Each activity also has a code which will target certain Futures Studies Goals and Characteristics of Foresight involved in the activity. In addition, the Characteristics of Foresight, The Ten Concepts, and other non-specified objectives are coded so the classroom teacher is aware of those factors inherent in each activity.

Below are the Goals of Futures Studies, Characteristics of Foresight, and the Ten Generic Concepts from Sections I and II. Since these items are referenced in each activity you may want to refer to them while building your lessons and targeting your intended student outcomes. In the beginning of each activity, the Futures Studies Goals and Characteristics of Foresight directly involved in the activity are marked by parentheses.

The Goals of Futures Studies

(1-Skill) Development of thinking skills and a conceptual framework necessary to understand complex systems.

(2-Skill) Development of abilities to identify and understand major trends and issues which will shape the future.

(3-Both) Development of an understanding of the nature of change and a means for coping with rapid change.

(4-Attitudinal) Development of more sophisticated and positive ways of thinking about alternative future possibilities.

The Characteristics of Foresight

1) A talented observer, who is sensitive to changes in his or her environs.

The development of this characteristic leads to identifying and understanding major trends and issues which are shaping our future.

2) A capable problem solver, who can piece together seemingly unrelated events/situations and able to recognize complex patterns.

Mastery of problem-solving calls for the development of higher order thinking skills, a conceptual understanding of systems, and a more holistic point of view.

3) A good data collector, who is familiar with many types of information bases and their delivery systems.

Tools which help us create, store, manipulate, and disseminate information will continue to drive our Information Age for some time to come. Familiarity with such systems will allow students to keep abreast of current information and knowledge.

4) A flexible and caring individual, who understands the nature of change and can develop sophisticated and positive ways of thinking about, coping with, and contributing to the future.

Change is projected as a long-range constant. Flexible thinking and the ability to create options are two essential coping skills we can give children.

The Ten Generic Concepts

Systems	Culture
Interdependence	Population
Change	Human Dignity
Conflict	Technology
Communication	Environment

SUGGESTED GRADE LEVEL: Upper Elementary -High School

ACITIVITY TITLE : *Local Explorers: Past, Present, Future*

GOALS INVOLVED: (1) (2) (3) 4 ALL

CHARACTERISTICS OF FORESIGHT INVOLVED: (1) (2) (3) 4 ALL

GENERIC CONCEPTS INVOLVED: Change, population, systems, interdependence, environment

ACTIVITIES/EXERCISES (facilitating goal accomplishment)

After obtaining a local road map of your community, discuss the following questions:

Is/was there a pattern to the growth of your community? How can you tell?

Why did growth happen in any pattern cited? (transportation routes, geographic/topographic features, etc.)

What are demographics and how can they help us better understand future patterns of growth and decline?

What are the demographics of your community? Have these demographics affected your community's growth? In what ways? How have the demographics of your community changed in the past 50 years, 100 years, etc. How do you think they will change in the future? Why?

What could you project as possible growth patterns for your community in the future? Why do you think these patterns will happen?

What is your community doing/not doing to insure growth in the future?

Does your community WANT growth in the future?

SENIOR HIGH STUDENTS START LOCALLY, THEN MOVE TO STATE AND NATIONAL MAPS.

ELEMENTARY STUDENTS: THIS STUDY COULD BE INCLUDED IN A UNIT ON THE COMMUNITY, OR SERVE AS A GUIDED STUDY WITHIN ANOTHER CURRICULAR AREA.

RESOURCES USED: Local/state/national road map

^^

EVALUATION:

____ Good ____ Satisfactory ____ Unsatisfactory (explain)____ Satisfactory with modification

LIST MODIFICATIONS/EXPLANATIONS ON THE BACK

SUGGESTEDGRADE LEVEL: Elementary-Middle School

ACTIVITY TITLE: *Creating a City of the Future*

GOALS INVOLVED: (1) (2) 3 (4) ALL

CHARACTERISTICS OF FORESIGHT INVOLVED: 1 (2) 3 (4) ALL

GENERIC CONCEPTS INVOLVED: System, Environment, Technology, Communication, Population, Interdependence

OTHER NON-SPECIFIED OBJECTIVES: Students working together as a group with a specific task to complete and then contribute to an even larger group effort.

ACTIVITIES/EXERCISES (facilitating goal accomplishment)

Begin by asking the class to brainstorm the different systems necessary to a city. Examples could be transportation, utilities, communication, health/medical, parks and recreation, etc.

After the major systems have been identified, ask the class to determine what approximate size (in terms of population) city they would like to use as the basis for the model they will build. The next question would be what approximate time in which this city would exist. The further out on a future horizon the city would exist, the less chance the systems they identified would resemble those in use today. For example, if the city will exist in the year 2050 there is a good chance the transportation system would be much less oriented toward cars, as we know them today, and oriented more toward some other method of future mass transportation.

Once the size and approximate time has been agreed upon, students should be divided into groups. Each group would be responsible for a specific system or projected need. Students in each group should be urged to do some research regarding how the system might operate, look, be made of (in the real life future), how its placement could impact on other city systems (use a Futures Wheel for this type of research).

The need for building material should be forecasted with plans outlined and coordinated with other groups so that the city would be a well-planned and coordinated effort. The "reality check" should be: "Is this a city in which I would want to live?" (See Activity #7 for a planning aid)

After plans have been drawn and coordinated, building materials should be gathered. Some examples of building materials could be L'eggs containers (one half of the container makes a great communication's satellite dish, especially with a toothpick glued to the center, the other half could be one of several domed agricultural centers) paper towel tubes, clear straws (for "vacuum bullet train" passages), etc. NOTE: Suggest to the students that of all geometric shapes known to us the square is the one which occurs the least in nature. Should this fact be reflected in the shapes of buildings? Why or why not?

^^^

EVALUATION:

____ Good ____ Satisfactory ____ Unsatisfactory (explain)____ Satisfactory with modification

LIST MODIFICATIONS/EXPLANATIONS ON THE BACK

SUGGESTED GRADE LEVEL: Middle School-High School

ACTIVITY TITLE: *Three Key Issues of the Future*

GOALS INVOLVED: 1 2 3 4 (ALL)

CHARACTERISTICS OF FORESIGHT INVOLVED: 1 (2) 3 (4) ALL

GENERIC CONCEPTS INVOLVED: Environment, Technology, Human Dignity, Population, Systems, Interdependence, Change, Conflict, Culture.

OTHER NON-SPECIFIED OBJECTIVES: Practice the problem-solving process and clarify attitudes toward the questions raised by the Three Key Issues.

ACTIVITIES/EXERCISES (facilitating goal accomplishment)

The **three key issues of the future focus on the** *environment, technology,* and *human dignity.* The way in which we choose to resolve these issues and their inherent problems will decide, in large part, what the quality of life will be for several generations to come.

A major element influencing the decision will be simply the number of inhabitants on the planet. The condition of our environment was not much of an issue until the recent past. There was abundant land and very limited global pollution problems until the industrial revolution was in high gear and fossil fuels were in wide-spread use. Of course, the amount of technology and level of technological complexity has increased commensurately with population levels.

Below are two opposing statements for each of the three key issues. Each statement is driven by certain attitudes. The attitudes, in turn, are a reflection of a set of values which promote certain actions.

Write the three sets of statements on the board and ask the following questions:

1) What are the attitudes behind each statement? 2) What are the consequences of each statement? \li360 \fi-360 3) If one statement was chosen over another how would it change you, your community, our country, the world?

4) How do attitudes drive, or promote, certain actions? 5) Which statements reflect what you believe in? Why?

ENVIRONMENT:

Statement #1: We have inherited the Earth from our forebearers.

Statement #2: We are borrowing the Earth from our children.

TEACHER NOTE: **What is the difference between inheriting and borrowing? Regarding time, are fore bearers part of the future or past? Are children part of the future or past? Why?**

TECHNOLOGY:

Statement #1: Technology is the major problem solving mechanism.

Statement #2: Technology creates more problems than it solves.

TEACHER NOTE: Could technology itself be neutral, and its application/use be values-loaded?

HUMAN DIGNITY:

Statement #1: All peoples of the Earth should have equal access to all resources of the Earth.

Statement #2: The western world has worked hard for its gains. The rest of the world could have our standard of living too if it would work for it.

TEACHER NOTE: Some have observed that statement #1 could trace its roots to the Bible i.e., sharing, treating another as oneself. Statement #2 could trace its roots to the western/ "Protestant work ethic."

These are difficult and timely questions which provide ample opportunities for problem solving and studying cause-effect. As these are major real-life questions with which humankind has grapled for centuries, it is not intended that there is a specific right answer. These questions are intended to sensitize students to the three key issues of the future and to demonstrate the difficulty of determining a "right answer" on issues that have so many ramifications for so many people.

^^

SUGGESTED GRADE LEVEL: Upper Elementary -High School

ACTIVITY TITLE: *Issues, Problems, Options, and Time*

GOALS INVOLVED: (1) 2 (3) (4) ALL

CHARACTERISTICS OF FORESIGHT INVOLVED: (1) (2) 3 (4) ALL

GENERIC CONCEPTS INVOLVED: Systems, Interdependence, Change

OTHER NON-SPECIFIED OBJECTIVES: To show the correlation between delaying solutions and the effect that early action has on people and the magnitude of the problem.

ACTIVITIES/EXERCISES (facilitating goal accomplishment)
Some problems we encounter as individuals, nations, or the world have a peculiar characteristic: they get worse as we postphone appropriate and effective solutions. Another characteristic of problems is that as they get larger, they tend to affect more people while simultaneously, the number of solutions available to solve the problem diminishes.

Variables = 1)# of people affected by problem

2)# of options available to "fix" problem

issue/event — —> problem — —> crisis — —> disaster

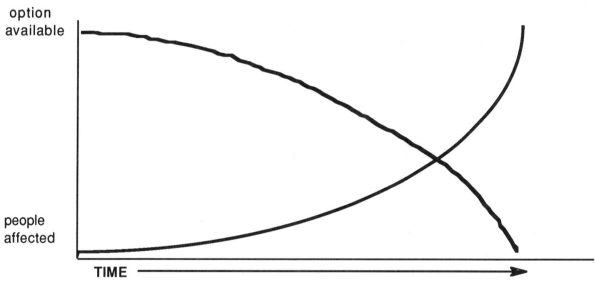

Activity: Start a log which examines local, state, or national situations which have grown to a threatening level. The newspaper is typically loaded with stories on such situations. After getting as many facts as possible on the situation, determine what causes allowed the situation to grow into a crisis or disaster. Some possible contributors might be: indifference/apathy, inadequate resources, ineffective leadership, and lack of communication of the problem. Make a bar graph showing the contributors and present to class while leading a discussion on this theme.
∧∧∧

EVALUATION:

____ Good ____ Satisfactory ____ Unsatisfactory (explain)____ Satisfactory with modification
LIST MODIFICATIONS/EXPLANATIONS ON THE BACK

SUGGESTED GRADE LEVEL: Upper Elementary -High School

ACTIVITY TITLE: *Interviewing: The Baby Boom's Past Present and Future*
GOALS INVOLVED: 1   2   3   4   (ALL)

CHARACTERISTICS OF FORESIGHT INVOLVED: (1) (2)   3   (4)   ALL

GENERIC CONCEPTS INVOLVED: Population, lifestyle, culture, change, technology.

ACTIVITIES/EXERCISES (facilitating goal accomplishment)

Baby Boom Backround Information

In a 17 year period, 1947-1964, 75 million babies were born in the United States. This group represents about one-third of the United States' population. People who study population (demographers) say this size of generation has never happened before in the history of the U.S., and will never happen again. The ramifications have been meaningful and will continue to be felt well into the next century. This phenomenon has, to a great degree, shaped marketing strategies, certain educational and governmental policies, given birth to billion dollar enterprises and generally reshaped our thinking toward several aspects of American life.

This phenomenon is the Baby Boom. The years between 1947-1964 are generally viewed as the baby boom years. Seventy-five million babies were born during this seventeen year period. Considering the fact that the U.S. only had a population of 150.7 million in 1950, 75 million babies being injected into the system was a significant event. These 75 million individuals represent the largest group of people to share a common temporal experience in the history of the United States. The baby boom cohort represents a demographic bulge with significantly smaller cohorts on either side. It has been likened to a "pig in a python"; an accurate graphic description of the large baby boom cohort, bordered on both sides by cohorts much smaller in size.

The baby boom has been, and will continue to be, an important influence on several elements of American society. While discussing the baby boom, one former director of the Bureau of the Census indicated the aging of the baby boom cohort will continue to be the major demographic factor well into the twenty-first century.

Below are examples of major changes made directly because of the baby boom. As mentioned above, the baby boom will continue to influence American culture well into the twenty-first century. If you can see just a glimpse of the changes already made by this cohort, it will help you to better understand the potential this group has for changing and shaping the future.

EXAMPLE 1

One of the many major affects of the procreation ethic and resultant baby boom was the large scale creation of the suburbs. More room and safer environments were necessary in which to raise children. Living in the urban areas was becoming too dangerous for the raising of children, something a little safer was needed. Also, adults were looking for less noisy and safer environs for their leisure-time. The suburban areas or "suburbs" amounted to a new cultural element in American life. Like the baby boom itself, the values, attitudes and interaction patterns found in the suburbs was an event which was difficult to match in U.S. history.

The dynamics of any society are often the same; as one problem is solved, a related problem emerges. In the suburbs one was living a distance from the center of business and schools. This made the second car a necessity..., preferably a small bus. Enter station wagons. Station wagons had existed before the baby boom, but they were a rarity. Now these wagons had a new and much larger calling. Other than getting to the grocery for food for all those children, there was a need for transportation to school and its myriad functions; also, social instruments such as the cub/boy/girl scouts, little league baseball, and various clubs beckoned to the teeming youth. The growing list of activities which resulted from this gigantic cohort seemed never ending.

The need for suburbs, the attendant infrastructure necessary to support suburbs, and the second automobile were some of the first major societal shifts caused by the baby boom, and they were made for each other—but this was only the beginning.

EXAMPLE 2

A new type of light began illuminating many of these suburban households. Instead of a regular element found in a light bulb, the light was emitted from a cathode ray tube first developed in the early thirties but not marketed with much success until the middle to late forties. This "new light" was a faithful baby sitter and was destined to be the baby boomers partner for life. This partnership is the type of association that results in large and long-lasting societal changes.

Perhaps television represents the best general barometer of what age spectrum (i.e. youth, middle aged, elderly) the baby boom cohort occupies. As a general rule, television producers and advertisers have consistently produced shows and advertised goods which appeal to this largest single market in the country; even the age of many of the actors, from situation-comedies to commercials, roughly correlates with the baby boomers' age brackets. When the cohort was young, shows were produced in response to their age and often became very popular. Walt Disney built an empire, the result of appealing to the tastes of a child-oriented society. One of Disney's many successes was the Davy Crockett series and the resultant marketing fad. In just seven months, the Davy Crockett market grossed more than 100 million 1955 dollars. (Jones, 1980, p.44) This was the largest television-baby boom marketing bonanza to that point and the economic potential of the baby boom has been shaping the American business sector ever since. Within the recent past, the Disney Studios came out with "Touchstone," a subsidiary movie enterprise which produces movies very much in line with, you guessed it, the baby boomers taste!

EXAMPLE 3

Another glowing illustration of the baby boom's economic ability is the success of the rock music industry. Retail sales figures for records went from $182 million in 1954 to $400 million in 1957 and then to $521 million in 1960 (Jones, 1980). The retail sales figures of this period of time were only a warm-up for the billion dollar sales yet to come.

The music made the culture of youth and the culture of youth made the music. As a larger percentage of the baby boomers moved into the "musically influenced" age, the retail sales figures continued to soar and increasing numbers of individuals rose to musical prominence almost overnight.

Along with record sales came more sophisticated equipment built to reproduce the sound. Finally, the very mode of music reproduction has evolved from 78's, to 45's, to "LP's," to 8 track tapes, to cassette tapes, to compact discs, to digital audio tapes. All this created many major audio equipment and audio related companies with no end in sight to the quest for "clean, clear, audio reproduction." Another illustration of the new consumerism mentioned earlier: new technology, change for change sake, built-in obsolescence..., Newer! Better!

1) Using your brainstorming skills only, list ways in which the U.S. was unprepared for the large number of births in the baby boom and the changes which had to be made to accommodate them. For example: more schools and teachers in the early 1950's, increased manufacturing and sales of baby furniture, baby food, etc.

2) Based on your brainstorming of question number 1 and the examples given above, create a "futures wheel" designed to determine in what ways life in the U.S. would have been different without the emergence of the baby boom? Enumerate, using several different first and second order examples.

3) Find some baby boomers to interview (remember there are over 75 million of them out there). Put together a list of questions dealing with their schooling (both their K-12 experience and college, if applicable), childhood dreams and expectations, adolescence, their experience with the Vietnam Conflict, and their current lives (i.e. Is it what you thought it would be? why/why not?). Try to find baby boomers who were born in the early boom (1947-1955) and the later, continuing boom (1956-64). Do their stories correlate? Are the same things emphasized? Why or why not? Finally, ask your interviewees what they believe the future holds for the baby boomers and vice versa. Put the results of your interviews into a report to share with the class.

^^^

EVALUATION:

____ Good ____ Satisfactory ____ Unsatisfactory (explain)____ Satisfactory with modification

LIST MODIFICATIONS/EXPLANATIONS ON THE BACK

SUGGESTED GRADE LEVEL: Upper Elementary-High School

ACTIVITY TITLE: *After Scenario Writing: Make an Audio-Visual Show!*

GOALS INVOLVED: 1 (2) 3 (4) ALL

CHARACTERISTICS OF FORESIGHT INVOLVED: 1 (2) (3) 4 ALL

GENERIC CONCEPTS INVOLVED: Communication, systems, technology.

OTHER NON-SPECIFIED OBJECTIVES: Allow students to work in a new medium to present information.

ACTIVITIES/EXERCISES (facilitating goal accomplishment)

(Note: if resources do not allow each student to make a slide-tape production, have them combine elements of several scenarios into a single scenario.)

1) Have students create a "story board" laying out the important elements of the scenario. If there are gaps, let them as a group, edit and develop parts to fill the gaps and make a smooth transition from one part of the scenario to another. Research will probably be necessary to insure factual realism and continuity of the story.

2) Once the story board is finished to the satisfaction of all, have students bring in magazines, etc., containing pictures which appropriately illustrate the story. *National Geographic, OMNI, The Futurist,* and year-end issues (i.e. "The Year in Pictures"), are excellent for this purpose. Students may also draw illustrations not otherwise available.

3) Ask your Media Center personnel to take slide photographs of the chosen pictures or, in the older grades, let student photographers do the same. (This could be one or more students' contribution to the product).

4) After the slides are developed, have students arrange the slides in a slide tray in a rough order while reading the narrative aloud (the text of the scenario). This step is to insure that, as the slides are being shown, the correct pictures come on at the proper time in the narrative. Refine the order until satisfied that the best picture is on at the appropriate time, based on what the narrative is saying. After this is done, number the slides.

5) If extra slides are needed, shoot and develop them, add to the other slides, and finalize the coordination of slides and narrative. Some type of mark should be put in the narrative where you want the slide to change to the next one. The coordination of the recorded narrative and slide arrangement should not leave any slide on the screen for too long. The audience will tire of the image and begin to lose interest.

6) Have students choose readers and record them reading the narrative. It goes without saying that the students be very familiar with the narrative script. The scenario readers cannot speak in a monotone voice..., add emotion when it is called for. Have the student readers practice reading the scenario narrative with a tape recorder so they may hear themselves and make necessary corrections before the final recording.

7) Do the final recording on a cassette tape recorder. All schools have (or have access to) a cassette tape recorder capable of placing inaudible cues on a cassette tape. This will automatically forward the slide tray at the proper time. The cues should then be placed on the tape at the point marked in #5 above. (A rule of thumb: no one slide should be on the screen for more than 9-12 seconds)

The icing on the cake:

After the slide arrangement and recording of the scenario narrative is done, you might explore the possibility of recording another sound track which contains only music. First, see if your District Media Center can combine the music and the narrative onto one cassette tape. Appropriate music, like the pictures can influence audiences in ways which the written scenario cannot.

RESOURCES NEEDED: Carousel projector, magazines, camera stand, inaudible cue machine, music, sound mixer.

^^^

EVALUATION:

____ Good ____ Satisfactory ____ Unsatisfactory (explain)____ Satisfactory with modification

LIST MODIFICATIONS/EXPLANATIONS ON THE BACK

SUGGESTED GRADE LEVEL: Upper Elememtary-High School

ACTIVITY TITLE: *What's the Plan!?*

GOALS INVOLVED: (1) (2) (3) 4 ALL

CHARACTERISTICS OF FORESIGHT INVOLVED: 1 (2) 3 (4) ALL

GENERIC CONCEPTS INVOLVED: Communication, systems, interdependence.

OTHER NON-SPECIFIED OBJECTIVES: Development of planning and decision-making skills.

ACTIVITIES/EXERCISES (facilitating goal accomplishment)

Being a good planner is one of the most sought after abilities you may possess. Below is a planning method which may help you become a good planner. You are invited to use this planning method on activity # 2, "Create a City of the Future."

The Seven Step Planning Method

1) Clarify the goal(s) you wish to achieve.

2) Estimate the resources available to you.

3) "Rough-out" some possible options/alternative plans available to you.

4) Try to predict any problems you might encounter in trying to reach the goal(s) in #1 above.

5) Choose the best optional plan available from #3 above.

6) Build-up the total plan, detail it in.

7) Critique the plan and make any necessary adjustments.

The Characteristics of a Good Plan

— The plan takes several different factors into consideration.

— Everyone involved, or playing a role, understands the plan.

— The plan is compatible with your needs, goals, resources-at-hand, etc.

— The plan is properly timed in terms of goals, needs, and support.

— The action called for by the plan is worth doing.

— The plan *will* work.

^^

EVALUATION:

____ Good ____ Satisfactory ____ Unsatisfactory (explain)____ Satisfactory with modification

LIST MODIFICATIONS/EXPLANATIONS ON THE BACK

SUGGESTED GRADE LEVEL: Middle School -High School

ACTIVITY TITLE: *What Do Futurists Believe?*

GOALS INVOLVED: 1 (2) 3 (4) ALL

CHARACTERISTICS OF FORESIGHT INVOLVED: (1) 2 3 (4) ALL

GENERIC CONCEPTS INVOLVED: Systems/interdependence, conflict, technology, human dignity.

ACTIVITIES/EXERCISES (facilitating goal accomplishment)

Below is a partial list of promient futurists. Find an article, part of a book, or a teacher hand-out written by, or about a futurist. Then analyze the reading by focusing on what the futurist's point-of-view on the future is and what the futurist's outlook is for the future. For example, some questions to help you analyze what the futurist's point of view might be:

1) Is the specific futurists' outlook positive or negative? Why?

2) Does the futurist include a world view or does their forecast focus on just one country?

3) What role does technology play in their outlook?

4) What is their outlook for the environment?

5) What is said about human dignity?

Roy Amara	Hazel Henderson
Issac Asimov	Bertrand de Jouvenal
Daniel Bell	Herman Kahn
Kenneth Boulding	Dennis Meadows
Arthur C. Clarke	Gerald K. O'Neill
Edward Cornish	John Platt
Amitai Etzioni	Fred Polak
Paul Ehrlich	Glenn T. Seaborg
Jay Forrester	Harold Shane
Buckminster Fuller	Robert Theobald
Willis Harman	Alvin Toffler

RESOURCES NEEDED:

Besides the *Reader's Guide to Periodical Literature* another helpful resource would be:

Coates, J. & Jarratt, J.; "What Futurists Believe," *The Futurist*, November-December 1990.

^^

EVALUATION:

____ Good ____ Satisfactory ____ Unsatisfactory (explain)____ Satisfactory with modification

LIST MODIFICATIONS/EXPLANATIONS ON THE BACK

SUGGESTED GRADE LEVEL: Middle School -High School

ACTIVITY TITLE: *What Causes Change?*

GOALS INVOLVED: 1 2 3 4 (ALL)

CHARACTERISTICS OF FORESIGHT INVOLVED: (1) (2) 3 (4) ALL

GENERIC CONCEPTS INVOLVED: Change, conflict, systems, interdependence.

OTHER NON-SPECIFIED OBJECTIVES: To reach an understanding that change doesn't "just happen." It is the result of "change drivers" which cause the change, although not always in a predictable way.

ACTIVITIES/EXERCISES (facilitating goal accomplishment)

There are six widely accepted factors which drive most change. Some factors produce change which is swift and overnight; some of the change is subtle and takes decades to finally be realized. As you read about each type of change think of examples of change caused by that factor in your own life or your community.

SIX CHANGE FACTORS

1) DEMOGRAPHIC CHANGE

Any population increase or decrease in size, or shift in the age or sex distribution sets other changes in motion. Examples of these changes would be birth and death rates, life expectancy, family size, balance of young vs. old within a society, and migration or mobility.

2) TECHNOLOGICAL CHANGE

Changes in technology lead to other changes. For example, a shift from ropes to horsecollars greatly increased the animals' ability to pull, leading to higher efficiency/productivity. Another example of the impact of technological change is the invention of an offset printing machine or faster computers with increased memory/storage capability.

3) SOCIAL INVENTION

The term "social" is used here in a broad sense to include the invention of new arrangements, systems or styles of educational, political, economic, religious, or military dimensions. Innovation here is more difficult to define than in the technological sphere, but would include new ways of organizing human effort (corporations), new political institutions (parliaments), different styles/arrangements of married couples, etc.

4) INFORMATION/IDEA SHIFTS

The scope, quantity, and manipulation of knowledge all fall within this category. Examples would include a scientific discovery, a new theory about child rearing, emerging conceptualizations regarding ourselves, the cosmos, and how the two interact..., also known as paradigm shifts, especially in science.

5) ENVIRONMENTAL CHANGE

Changes in society/civilization may be caused by environmental change. Earthquakes, major flooding of a habitat, volcanoes, forest fires, etc. can all affect and change populations. The causes of this change are structural in nature and humankind usually has little choice but to adapt.

6) CULTURAL/VALUE SHIFTS

All cultures have a set of unspoken values/norms. Changes in cultural axioms or values may trigger other important changes. An example of a changed cultural assumption: the somewhat unnoticed shift in the way Man used time after the coming of industrialism: carefully conditioned habits of punctuality, synchronizing of men's schedules with the machines availability. An example of a recent value shift: decreased pre-marital sex/promiscuous in U.S. due primarily to fear of disease and increased religious/moral pursuits.

— From newspapers and magazines, identify examples of each change factor in operation. Bring this information to school and share with your class.

— Start a log or scrapbook with six different sections; one for each change factor. Place information such as magazine/newspaper clippings in the proper section. Also, write in your own observations of change occuring because of one of the six factors identified above.

— Write a report which is your analysis of the six different types of change. Include the illustrations (and your own observations) which you have found over a three month period. Take the report and share it with your class. Also, ask your teacher and /or parents to help you find a different audience for your report; your local newspaper for example.

^^

EVALUATION:

____ Good ____ Satisfactory ____ Unsatisfactory (explain)____ Satisfactory with modification

LIST MODIFICATIONS/EXPLANATIONS ON THE BACK

SUGGESTED GRADE LEVEL: Middle School - High School

ACTIVITY TITLE: *Using the Ten Generic Concepts*

GOALS INVOLVED: 1   2   3   4   (ALL)

CHARACTERISTICS OF FORESIGHT INVOLVED: (1)   (2)   3   4   ALL

TEN CONCEPTS INVOLVED: All

OTHER NON-SPECIFIED OBJECTIVES: An opportunity for analysis of written material and synthesis of new relationships.

ACTIVITIES/EXERCISES (facilitating goal accomplishment)

Ask each student to choose one of the Ten Generic Concepts (See Section II) for investigation;

1) Then find an article in a periodical or media presentation of some sort which relates in some direct way to the chosen concept;

2) Next, analyze the resource by:

   a) Identifying the thesis the author has developed,
   b) Noting the data presented to support or refute the thesis,
   c) Recording how the issue could impact on the future and,
   d) Identify other unique characteristics about the concept being studied.

3) Finally, students should specify how each of the issue(s) from the article relates to the other concepts.

NOTE: An excellent periodical if your library/media center does not already carry it is The World Future Society's journal, *The Futurist*. This is especially appropriate for high school students but middle school students have also used it for research projects.

RESOURCES USED: Periodicals and media presentations

^^

EVALUATION:

____ Good ____ Satisfactory ____ Unsatisfactory (explain)____ Satisfactory with modification

LIST MODIFICATIONS/EXPLANATIONS ON THE BACK

SUGGESTED GRADE LEVEL: Upper Elementary High School

ACTIVITY TITLE: *Creating Your Future*

GOALS INVOLVED: 1 2   3   4   (ALL)

CHARACTERISTIC OF FORESIGHT: 1 (2) 3 (4)   ALL

GENERIC CONCEPTS INVOLVED: Lifestyle, culture, human dignity, systems, interdependence.

OTHER NON-SPECIFIED OBJECTIVES: To characterize basic personal needs and extrapolate those needs.

ACTIVITIES/EXERCISES (facilitating goal accomplishment)

The "think sheet" below is a quick and easy way to structure this activity. Dr. Carl Keener of Ball State University was the creator. This activity can serve as a springboard for discussion and personalizing attitudes which may reflect a futurist's stance.

THINK SHEET

How does someone go about preparing to live in the future? The person who will be truly ready to make inroads toward creating his or her future must first decide what is important to them in the future. Whereas it is true the individual may have little or nothing to say about some things in the future (especially those in the immediate future) the individual can have influence on desired long- range futures, even on a global basis, if the individual plans for it.

Step One: Carefully think about your seven basic needs.

Every human being has a built-in capacity to fulfill the self. The basic human needs are the needs of the: 1) **body** (health, vigor, sensual pleasure); 2) **mind** (knowledge, understanding, wisdom, creativity), 3) **character** (virtue, justice, dignity, honesty, human rights); 4) **community** (brotherhood, rights of others, benevolence); 5) **politics** (peace, civil liberty); 6) **economics** (health, wages, access to educational facilities for improvement, free time) and 7) **society** (status, equality in life for a person). *This will take some time to really analyze one's needs, NOT simply his or her wants. Needs and wants are not the same.*

Step Two: Keeping in mind what your basic needs are, think how they will be met in the year 1999. After thinking about this describe briefly how each of your seven needs will be met.

Step Three: Now think ahead to the year 2009. Describe briefly how each of your seven needs will be met then.

Step Four: Now, really think future!! Briefly describe the future you want when you are 40 years old. Describe your personal situation and your perception of the global situation. Also, describe how can you work now to promote the more positive things and avoid the negative.

^^^

EVALUATION:

____ Good ____ Satisfactory ____ Unsatisfactory (explain)____ Satisfactory with modification

LIST MODIFICATIONS/EXPLANATIONS ON THE BACK

SUGGESTED GRADE LEVEL: All

ACTIVITY TITLE: *Examining the Decision-Making Process*

GOALS INVOLVED: 1   (2)   (3)   (4)   ALL

CHARACTERISTICS OF FORESIGHT INVOLVED: 1   2   3   4   (ALL)

GENERIC CONCEPTS INVOLVED: Communication, conflict, systems.

ACTIVITIES/EXERCISES (facilitating goal accomplishment)

Experience has nothing to do with correctness in decision making. To become an experienced decision maker, it helps if you understand the actual process involved.

The decision-making process involves three steps:

Experimental evaluation: This step involves using divergent thinking or brainstorming to seek alternative solutions. It also involves brainstorming for the conditions existing in each alternative solution/option, the limitations of each, and the probable effects of each choice, and under certain conditions, the ulterior motives of each option.

Logical evaluation: This step involves convergent thinking to narrow possible solutions down to the best possible one or two options upon which to base the decision. This process would be based on answering the following questions: what are the main goals, what will be accomplished by choosing each option, and how to best implement the decsion.

Judgement: This is the key step.   Evaluate the options in terms of **your** alternatives, conditions and goals. Make the decision. Implement what is called for.

Any properdecision-making process must include:

  —A thorough examination/discussion of the situation driving the need for a decision.
  —An examination of the pro's and con's of each decision.
  —A weighing of the pro's and con's of each decision.
  —Coming to a conclusion.
  —Being able to defend the final decision.

—Find a magazine or newspaper article which deals with a recent decision affecting the future. Examine as much information as possible about the decision and go through the above process. Let students then determine if they would come up with the same decision and then ask why they either did or did not chose the same option.

^^^

EVALUATION:

____ Good ____ Satisfactory ____ Unsatisfactory (explain)____ Satisfactory with modification

LIST MODIFICATIONS/EXPLANATIONS ON THE BACK

SUGGESTED GRADE LEVEL: Middle School -High School

ACTIVITY TITLE: *The King and his Daughter: Exponential Growth*

GOALS INVOLVED: 1 (2) (3) (4) ALL

CHARACTERISTICS OF FORESIGHT INVOLVED: (1) (2) 3 4 ALL

GENERIC CONCEPTS INVOLVED: Population, systems, environment.

OTHER NON-SPECIFIED OBJECTIVES: To understand the nature of exponential growth and its impact on ourselves and our world.

ACTIVITIES/EXERCISES (facilitating goal accomplishment)

The following story is an adaptation illustrating the nature of exponential growth. It could be an old Chinese fairy tale—nevertheless, it is an excellent way to illustrate the nature of exponential growth.

Once upon a time there lived a king and his beautiful daughter in a glorious kingdom by the sea. One day while walking in the woods the daughter was captured by an ugly, foul-breathed, fire- breathing, knock-kneed, hard of hearing, dragon. The dragon took the princess to his home where he intended to cut her up into tiny, tiny, pieces unless the U.N. freed a number of dragons being kept inside the Appalachian Mountains. The king was terribly upset—**he** wasn't part of the U.N. and he had never even laid eyes on a dragon. He advertised high and low to grant the wish of anyone who could save his beloved daughter from this terrible, terrorist plight.

An individual, not unlike a famous movie star who fights terrorists, heard of the offer and set about finding the princess and bringing the dragon to justice. As usual, he captured the dragon, saved the princess and returned her to the king. The king, who was so delighted to have his daughter back offered to grant any wish the man made. Of all the things he could have asked for, the man ask for a grain of rice!!!

Since rice was one of the major exports of the country, the king was more than happy to grant the wish. However, the man's full wish had not yet been heard. He said he would return for more rice each day for as many days as there are squares on a chess board. Each day he returned he would receive double the number of grains of rice than on the previous day. The king merrily agreed, gave him his grain of rice, and told the valet to bring his car.

The next day the man knocked on the front door of the castle and received his two grains of rice— the third day he came to recieve his four grains of rice and bid farewell. This continued for about a month until one day the king met the man at the front door and had him assassinated. WHY??

To solve this problem and answer associated questions, students will need the following approximate conversions. They might also like to draw a grid on a piece of paper which will represent the squares on a chess board.

- 131,072 grains of rice = 1 box of rice
- 1,024 boxes = 1 ton
- Total rice harvest of the entire world = approximately 350 million tons

58

Now that students have this data, present them with the following questions:

1) Why did the king kill the young man?

2) Make a graph of the increase in rice grains/tons per day. What problems do you encounter?

3) What is exponential growth and how does it relate to this story?

4) Give examples of exponential growth in the world today.

5) How can exponential growth be a threat to our environment?

6) In what way(s) could you use exponential growth to forecast the future?

^^

EVALUATION:

____ Good ____ Satisfactory ____ Unsatisfactory (explain)____ Satisfactory with modification

LIST MODIFICATIONS/EXPLANATIONS ON THE BACK

SUGGESTED GRADE LEVEL: Upper Elementary -Middle School

ACTIVITY TITLE: *Creating a Survey Study of Your School*

GOALS INVOLVED: (1) (2) 3 (4) ALL

CHARACTERISTICS OF FORESIGHT INVOLVED: (1) 2 (3) (4) ALL

GENERIC CONCEPTS INVOLVED: Communication, change, lifestyle.

OTHER NON-SPECIFIED OBJECTIVES: To sharpen surveying skills and to enhance the students ability to work cooperatively in groups.

ACTIVITIES/EXERCISES (facilitating goal accomplishment)

Since not all schools have courses which deal with some aspect of the future it is sometimes interesting to do a survey to see if students are even thinking about the future in any positive, creative way. The following survey was created by Gil Caudill (a private therapist working with gifted children) to determine just how much time and interest students exhibit toward the future.

SURVEY OF INTEREST IN THE FUTURE

Grade level: _____   **Age:** _____

1. I think about future world situations _____% each week.
2. I think about future personal situations _____% each week.
3. I think about solutions to future world problems _____% each week.
4. I think about solutions to future personal problems _____% each week.
5. I know what _____% of my future will be.
6. I would like to know _____% of my future.
7. I see "glimpses/images" of the future _____% of the time.
8. I want to see into the future _____% of the time.
9. I want to think about the future _____% of the time.
10. I want to consider future possibilities _____% of the time.

The class should be divided into the following working groups: delivery/collection, tallying information, and "statistics." The last two tasks: analysis and report, should include everyone.

The responsiblities of each group involve:

Delivery/collection: This step involves writing a letter to other teachers. In this letter you would tell them what the class is doing and asking if surveys could be brought to their room **at their convenience** during a certain time period for their students to complete. Upon receiving the replies this group would then set up a delivery schedule, deliver the surveys, wait for their completion, answer any questions, and bring them back to the room.

Information Tallying: Once the forms are back this group compiles a list of all the responses to each item. When done, each item (except grade level and age) will have a list of percentages given by each student on each question.

Statistics: This group takes the tallies done by the "Information Tallying" group and finds the mean percentage on each question. Of more interest might be the range of percentages for each question and the median percentage for each question. Determine if there are broad differences in responses between grade levels and/or age groupings.

Analysis and Report: After the statistics are available they should be written on the board so the entire class will see the results. A class discussion could then emerge in which class members compare and contrast the differing results and come up with statements which sum up the survey results. Once the summary statements are finished and agreed upon, the report may begin with a group taking one of the ten questions and writing it up. Once all groups are finished, the write ups may be compiled into a complete report.

^^^

EVALUATION:

____ Good ____ Satisfactory ____ Unsatisfactory (explain)____ Satisfactory with modification

LIST MODIFICATIONS/EXPLANATIONS ON THE BACK

SUGGESTED GRADE LEVEL: Senior High

ACTIVITY TITLE: *Surveying Student Perceptions of the Future*

GOALS INVOLVED: (1)   (2)   3   (4)   ALL

CHARACTERISTICS OF FORESIGHT INVOLVED: (1)   2   (3)   (4)   ALL

GENERIC CONCEPTS INVOLVED: Communication, change, lifestyle.

OTHER NON-SPECIFIED OBJECTIVES: To sharpen surveying skills and work cooperatively in task groups.

ACTIVITIES/EXERCISES (facilitating goal accomplishment)

Design a survey to see what students are thinking about the future. The following survey is suggested as a possible model upon which you may base your survey. Typically in this exercise, at this grade level, students want to personalize their survey efforts by coming up with their own questions about the future.

The suggested survey uses a five point Likert Scale and was created by the Futures Studies class at the 1990 Florida Governor's Summer College to determine what the "futures think" of the student population actually was.

SURVEY OF INTEREST IN THE FUTURE

Please Circle Your Grade level: 9   10   11   12

SA (strongly agree), A (agree), ? (don't know), D (disagree), SD (strongly disagree)

	SA	A	?	D	SD
1.) Capital punishment will become a nationwide policy by 2010.					
2.) A limited/regional nuclear war will occur by 2010.					
3.) Within 50 years, desalinization will become our primary means of obtaining water.					
4.) All drugs will be legalized on a global basis by 2040.					
5.) A single global economic community (similar to the European Economic Council) will form by 2040.					
6.) Terra-forming, the creation of an environment capable of supporting life, will permit us to live on other planets, etc. by 2040.					
7.) Sexually transmitted diseases (specifically AIDS) will eventually limit population.					
8.) Complete genetic control and regulation will be imposed on future generations by 2040.					

SA	A	?	D	SD

9.) Due to greater advancements in the use and safety of nuclear energy, we will eliminate pollution resulting from fossil fuels.

10.) Life expectancy will naturally decrease; a result of over-population.

11.) Humankind will be forced to live underground, undersea, or in space by 2040.

12.) At current rates of deterioration, the ozone layer will not be able to sufficiently deflect ultraviolet rays causing damage in different parts of the world.

13.) Eradication of diseases will happen by 2040.

14.) Due to uncontrolled birth rates the Earth's resources will not be able to satisfy human demands by 2040.

The class should be divided into the following working groups: question design delivery/collection, tallying information, and statistics. For the last two tasks: analysis and report, all should take part. The responsiblities of each group involve:

Question Design: This group surveys the class for areas of interest. Once they know what questions the entire class wants to ask, they design the questions, paying attention to clarity and realizing the "questions" are actually statements with which the respondents agree or disagree.

Delivery/collection: Putting together a letter to other teachers telling them what the class is doing and that you would like to bring the surveys to their room at their convenience during a certain time for their students. Upon receiving the replies the students set up a delivery schedule, deliver the surveys, wait for their completion by the students, and bring them back.

Information Tallying: When the surveys are returned this group makes a list of all the various responses to each item. When done, each item (except grade level and any other demographics the class might want to know), will have a list of percentages given by each student on each question.

Statistics: This group takes the tallies done by the Information Tallying group and finds the mean percentage on each question. Of added interest might be the range of percentages for each question and the median percentage for each question, etc. It is interesting to see if there are broad differences in responses between grade levels and/or age groupings.

Analysis and Report: After the statistics are available; they should be written on the board so the entire class may see the results. A class discussion could then be had in which class members may compare and contrast differing results and come up with statements which sum up the survey results. Once the summary statements are finished and agreed upon, the report should begin with a group taking one of the questions and writing it up. When all groups have finished their write ups, they may be compiled into a general report.

^^^

EVALUATION:

____ Good ____ Satisfactory ____ Unsatisfactory (explain)____ Satisfactory with modification

LIST MODIFICATIONS/EXPLANATIONS ON THE BACK

SUGGESTED GRADE LEVEL: Elementary

ACTIVITY TITLE: *"Futurizing with Rip Van Winkle"*

GOALS INVOLVED: 1 2 3 4 (ALL)

CHARACTERISTICS OF FORESIGHT INVOLVED: (1) (2) 3 (4) ALL

GENERIC CONCEPTS INVOLVED: Communication, culture, environment, systems, technology.

OTHER NON-SPECIFIED OBJECTIVES: Preparing for scenario writing through using only one's imagination.

ACTIVITIES/EXERCISES (facilitating goal accomplishment)

After reading/listening to a tape of the Rip Van Winkle classic, discuss the trip into the future of Rip Van Winkle.

What did it feel like for Van Winkle to awaken from such a long sleep and find himself in the future?

What could Rip have done to make the future feel more comfortable?

Have the students pretend that they have done something similar — fallen asleep for a long period of time (i.e. 25 years, 50 years, 100 years, etc.). They awaken to find themselves in the same place (their community) but at some future point in time. Through writing, ask the students to describe the scene.

— What changes have taken place in terms of: housing, transportation, food, clothing, entertainment, education, communications, and so on.

— To what age are people living? Why?

— What has happened regarding exciting medical innovations?

— Describe some people you meet. What are they thinking? With what are they concerned?

— After describing the changes they see ask the students to tell of their plan to adapt to the future. What problems do/will they meet and why? Likewise, what successes do they experience?

RESOURCES: The story (or tape) of the children's classic: *Rip Van Winkle* & some imagination/ creativity

^^^

EVALUATION:

____ Good ____ Satisfactory ____ Unsatisfactory (explain)____ Satisfactory with modification

LIST MODIFICATIONS/EXPLANATIONS ON THE BACK

SUGGESTED GRADE LEVEL: All

ACTIVITY TITLE: *Designing a Student Simulation About the Future*

GOALS INVOLVED: 1 2 (3) (4) ALL

CHARACTERISTICS OF FORESIGHT INVOLVED: 1 (2) 3 (4) ALL

GENERIC CONCEPTS INVOLVED: Change, communication, conflict, human dignity.

ACTIVITIES/EXERCISES (facilitating goal accomplishment)

Some of the most interesting simulations are those designed by the students themselves. The following is a "roadmap" which students may use in designing their own simulations. After they are finished the class can be an excellent "field test" for the simulation. The following items must be addressed in any simulation:

1) The name of the simulation.

2) The statement of the problem(s) which the simulation is trying to address or solve.

3) The simulation objectives (what is supposed to happen, and briefly, why?).

4) The setting: a description of backround information, where the simulation takes place, the approximate time setting, and any conditions which may effect the playing of the game.

5) A description of the characters and their circumstances. What are the vested interests of these people and what are their ultimate goals?

6) What resources will be needed to play the game?

7) The rules of the simulation: how is the game scored? How should the players act? By whom, or how are the rules to be implemented?

8) The evaluation and debriefing process: Were the goals and objectives reached? How can the simulation be improved?

RESOURCES USED: Any resources mentioned in #6 above.

TEACHER NOTE: Activity #30; "Not In My Backyard," can serve as a model for this exercise.

^^

EVALUATION:

____ Good ____ Satisfactory ____ Unsatisfactory (explain)____ Satisfactory with modification

LIST MODIFICATIONS/EXPLANATIONS ON THE BACK

SUGGESTED GRADE LEVEL: Middle School -Senior High

ACTIVITY TITLE: *Using Technology Assessment on the Cloning Issue*

GOALS INVOLVED: 1   2   3   4   (ALL)

CHARACTERISTICS OF FORESIGHT INVOLVED: (1)   (2)   3   (4)   ALL

GENERIC CONCEPTS INVOLVED: Technology, human dignity, population, culture.

ACTIVITIES/EXERCISES (facilitating goal accomplishment)

Technology assessment is a method of determining the effects upon society that may happen when a technology is introduced, extended or modified. It seeks to examine the unintended, indirect, or delayed consequences. Technology assessment allows us to "look around the corner" and anticipate possible outcomes of certain situations in order to plan for a better, more preferable future.

Clone: a group of organisms derived from a single individual by various means of asexual reproduction. (Ref: *Random House Dictionary)*

The cloning of organisms has long been a reality. For some time now scientists have been able to clone several mammals such as mice, rats, and even cattle. The cloning of human beings is possible. It is a relatively simple procedure in which the DNA (the "blueprint" for an organism) contained in an egg is replaced with the DNA of another organism and replaced to mature to term.

As a society (and civilization) we have chosen NOT to clone human beings. There are some obvious ethical and moral questions having no uniform, acceptable, answer at this point in time. Your class has been asked to assess the impacts of this technology within the context of cloning humans. There are nine steps involved in this method:

1) Structuring the problem: what exactly is the problem the technology is to alleviate?
2) Determining possible affects: if implemented as proposed, what would happen?
3) Evaluating affects: determining the benefits and liabilities of the technologies implementation.
4) Identifying the decision makers involved: who/what agency will determine the final yes or no?
5) Identifying vested interests and ultimate goals of the decision makers.
6) Identifying possible choices for the decision makers: are other possibilities available?
7) Identifying the stakeholders; the parties which have an interest: on whom will the technology impact—directly or indirectly, good or bad?
8) Determining conclusions, recommendations and modifications 9) Presentation of the results.

^^ ^^^^^^^^^^^^^^^^^^^^^^^^^

EVALUATION:

____ Good ____ Satisfactory ____ Unsatisfactory (explain)____ Satisfactory with modification

LIST MODIFICATIONS/EXPLANATIONS ON THE BACK

SUGGESTED GRADE LEVEL: Elementary -Middle School

ACTIVITY TITLE: *Writing Utopias*

GOALS INVOLVED: (1) 2 3 (4) ALL

CHARACTERISTICS OF FORESIGHT INVOLVED: 1 (2) 3 (4) ALL

GENERIC CONCEPTS INVOLVED: Communication, systems, change, culture, population, environment.

OTHER NON-SPECIFIED OBJECTIVES: To sharpen creative writing skills, develop an optimistic view of certain possible futures, and to aid in preparation for scenario writing.

ACTIVITIES/EXERCISES (facilitating goal accomplishment)

Utopias describe a place of political and social perfection. Humankind has always pursued this dream of perfection. To reach some semblance of a Utopia one must first visualize it. Writing Utopias is a step in this direction. After explaining the nature of Utopia, ask the students to write a Utopia including information about as many following factors as possible:

GOVERNMENT	NATURAL RESOURCES
LEISURE	EDUCATION
ENERGY SOURCES	COMMUNICATION
TECHNOLOGY	ECOLOGY
HUMAN RELATIONSHIPS	TRANSPORTATION
FOOD SOURCES	MEDICAL/HEALTH CARE

After the students have finished they could get into groups and combine elements of each group members Utopia into one larger Utopia. Next, the students should become so familiar with their Utopia that they could role-play the part of a citizen from the Utopia described. As a finishing touch, you could arrange for a video camera to tape segments of an interview with members of the various Utopias in a "man-on-the-street" format.

Students could also be placed in groups to work on the development of Utopias in currently undeveloped regions of the Earth such as Antarctica and Greenland. Perhaps the "United Nations Development Committee" has asked the particular groups to plan developments in various areas of the lanet and make a formal report on the finished plan.

RESOURCES USED: Video camera

^^^

EVALUATION:

____ Good ____ Satisfactory ____ Unsatisfactory (explain)____ Satisfactory with modification

LIST MODIFICATIONS/EXPLANATIONS ON THE BACK

SUGGESTED GRADE LEVEL: Upper Elementary -Middle School

ACTIVITY TITLE: *Investigative Reporters: Change in the Last 50 Years*

GOALS INVOLVED: 1   2   3   4   (ALL)

CHARACTERISTICS OF FORESIGHT INVOLVED: (1)   (2)   3   (4)   ALL

GENERIC CONCEPTS INVOLVED: Change, technology, systems, communication, culture, environment.

OTHER NON-SPECIFIED OBJECTIVES: To learn more about the nature and rate of change and to practice the interview method of information gathering.

ACTIVITIES/EXERCISES (facilitating goal accomplishment)

There are several ways to determine change over time. You may read about it, watch movies and/or videotapes, interview people who have lived longer than you, or observe it in your own life. The best way to get a comprehensive picture of change is to use a number of these methods, especially the interview. Some of the best, most personal, points of view come from interviewing people older than we are. They have knowledge of events we can only read about.

Contact some people who are older, maybe your grandparents, and ask them about the following topics:

1) Transportation — How has transportation changed in their lifetime? Are there different modes of transportation available now that were not available when they were children. What about the speed of transportation? Is it **ultimately** (i.e., traffic jams, cancelled flights, etc.) faster, slower? What about the comfort in current transportation modes as opposed to those of the past? How has technology helped/hindered transportation? What have been the impacts on the environment? Is transportation generally better or worse than in the past?

2) Housing — How does current housing differ from the housing of their youth? Is it bigger or smaller. Are the lot sizes about the same? Are there more apartments now than in the past? Are building materials different? What about the "things" we put in the housing, such as TV's, VCR's, stereo systems, microwave ovens, etc. how different are they and what are they supposed to do for the owners today that is different from what was available in the past? What about the cost of housing today? How has technology helped/hindered housing? What have been the impacts on the environment? Overall, is housing better or worse than in the past?

3) Family — How have families changed in their lifetime? Are they bigger or smaller? Why do they think families are bigger or smaller? What about the idea of both parents working outside the home? Is this good or bad? Why? Many families are spread out across the United States now; Is that the same or different from when your interviewee was young? Is this good or bad, and why? How has technology helped/hindered the family?   In general, is the family in better or worse shape than in the past?

4) Clothing/Cosmetics — How has clothing/cosmetics changed in terms of: 1) styles, 2) materials used, 3) cost, and 4) what is acceptable on what age of individual (i.e. should 5th graders wear lipstick, etc.)? Why does clothing change so much? How has technology helped/hindered clothing/cosmetics? What have been the impacts on the environment? (At one point, an element found in mascara & eye liner came from whales) Overall, is the clothing/ cosmetic industry better or worse than in the past?

5) Values — What was acceptable behavior for youth in the past? How do they feel about today's youth? Are they essentially the same or different? Why? What do they suppose is the reason for the change? Ask them to give examples. How has technology helped/hindered values in America? How has the environment been effected? Are the values in this society generally better or worse than in the past?

Now switch your perspective to the future and ask the person you are interviewing what he or she think will happen to each of the above topics in the next ten, twenty-five, and forty years.?

Remember the further out into the future one looks, the more change there is possible (See the "caveat" mentioned in the Trend Extrapolation tool in Section IV). On this part of the activity you might also want to ask your parents, friends, and also include your own forecasts of what might occur based on the information you have gathered.

Summarize the information you have gathered on these topics into a report. Are there any patterns to the responses? Are the reasons for change the same or different? Look at Activity #9. Which of the six reasons for change are involved in the different topics in your report?

^^^

EVALUATION:

____ Good ____ Satisfactory ____ Unsatisfactory (explain)____ Satisfactory with modification

LIST MODIFICATIONS/EXPLANATIONS ON THE BACK

69

SUGGESTED GRADE LEVEL: Elementary -Middle School

ACTIVITY TITLE: *"If It's To Be, Its Up To Me"*

GOALS INVOLVED: 1   2   (3)   (4)   ALL

CHARACTERISTICS OF FORESIGHT INVOLVED: (1)   2   3   (4)   ALL

GENERIC CONCEPTS INVOLVED: Change, environment, communication.

OTHER NON-SPECIFIED OBJECTIVES: To learn the potential of mental imaging in planning one's life and future.

ACTIVITIES/EXERCISES (facilitating goal accomplishment)

In our minds, each of us has what some people call "movies of the mind." They are: 1) images of past events, 2) mental translations of current situations, and 3) bridges helping us to get from where we are now to where we want to be in the future. These mental images of the past, present, and future are very helpful to us. It is important for us to build healthy images of "ourself-in- the-future." This activity will concentrate on the mental images of the present and future.

> Future expectations of one's self motivates current student behavior. "An even more powerful motivational force is a person's vision or image of himself or herself in the future—expectations of what persons will become relative to what they are in the present are considered powerful determinants of behavior." (Torrance, 1979b; Torrance & Hall, 1980) "Futurists,... are strong advocates of such imaging by individuals. They believe that persons' images of themselves in the future can only lead them to strive for its actualization. There is much to be said for this, and educators must be alert to the task of preparing.... students to use this significant motivational mechanism." (Khatena, 1982, p. 303)

When children image, they learn to focus on these movies in their mind and determine what meaning, or call to action, the mental images might be suggesting. With practice and assistance, they can be more in-tune with their own perceptions.

1) Tell the students they are going to take a short trip into the future to see what they are doing there. Then spend a few minutes in a relaxation exercise.

2) After the relaxation exercise tell the students to let their minds "wander."

3) Give a focusing phrase or word (mnemonic device) for the students to image: a sunny, warm island beach, a high meadow in the mountains, etc.

4) Tell the students to wander into this picture they have created as their adult-self.

5) Then the students should introduce themselves to their adult-self and prepare for a pleasant talk.

6) After the "talk" with their adult, future-selves the students should slowly come back from their imaging exercise and write of the experience.

70

Certain questions should be ask to help the students clarify their imaging exercise:

1) How did you enjoy your talk? Was it fun talking with yourself as an adult?

2) Did you enjoy yourself as an adult? Why or why not?

3) What did you do for a career as an adult? How many careers had you already had? What other careers did you still wish to experience?

4) What were some of the events your adult-self had experienced?

5) What can you start doing now to assure you become/don't become that person?

This list of questions is by no means inclusive. They are good starter questions. You will know your class/group very well and will know other questions which may be appropriate for your students. You are invited to "tailor" questions based on this experience.

^^^

EVALUATION:

____ Good ____ Satisfactory ____ Unsatisfactory (explain)____ Satisfactory with modification

LIST MODIFICATIONS/EXPLANATIONS ON THE BACK

71

SUGGESTED GRADE LEVEL: Middle School -High School

ACTIVITY TITLE: *The Futurist's Schools of Thought*

GOALS INVOLVED: 1   2   3   4   (ALL)

CHARACTERISTICS OF FORESIGHT INVOLVED: (1) (2) 3 (4)   ALL

GENERIC CONCEPTS INVOLVED: Systems, interdependence, change, technology, human dignity, environment.

OTHER NON-SPECIFIED OBJECTIVES: To examine the differences between the futurists' schools of thought and gain a clearer understanding of what Futurists are saying about the future.

ACTIVITIES/EXERCISES (facilitating goal accomplishment)

THE FUTURIST'S SCHOOLS OF THOUGHT6

In this activity we will focus on the several differences between futurists and why they view the future in such opposite ways. By examining and understanding the differences between the various futurist's schools of thought, you will gain a much clearer understanding of *what* they are saying about the future, and more important, why they are saying it. There are three basic schools of thought (and important sub-divisions): the extrapolists, the visionaries, and the client-centered.

THE EXTRAPOLISTS

A trend is a general pattern of events which has the tendency to occur in a specific direction over time. Trends may be short or long-term and may either increase or decrease in size. Trend extrapolation looks at the past history and characteristics of the trend(s) and projects those characteristics into the future. It is a simple, linear projection with little concern for outside or possible unforeseen factors which might influence the trend. For example: "If there has been increasing pollution of the environment in the past, given no intervention, we may expect pollution to increase in the future—possibly to the point that our natural system can no longer cleanse itself by natural processes."

Both the Negative and Positive Extrapolists choose trends and historical data as the base for their projections. The key differences lie in the type of trends they choose and the type of "certainties" upon which they base their forecasts. The following outline will indicate the key assumptions, methodologies, and values for the two types of extrapolists.

POSITIVE EXTRAPOLISTS

The positive extrapolists acknowledge problems in the world but believe that we can improve life for all by continued use of technology. They point to the fascinating things technology has done for Humankind in the past, such as antibiotics, genetic engineering, and atomic energy.

Continued growth is important whether it is in technology, population, or industrialization. The Positive Extrapolists feel there is a limit to certain types of growth, but the limitation is on a distant horizon, not immediate. Current government policy which promotes growth is considered good because all the benefits that have accrued to Humankind have been a result of past successful economic policies. The policies worked in the past, they will work in the future: extrapolation.

Positive Extrapolists believe:

—The optimistic trendscited by this group are based on "subjective certainties," or Laws of Man which are flexible, changable, modifiable.
—The current policyapproaches of governments are considered to be the best possible,
—Technologyis considered both good and the major problem-solving mechanism for problems,
—Growth(economic, industrial) is considered good,
—Global equityis not a pressing concern,
—Continuous progress is considered inevitable if left to expert decision makers.

NEGATIVE EXTRAPOLISTS

Negative Extrapolists are the opposite of Positive Extrapolists in most everything. They often focus their work on structural or natural systems whereas the Positive Extrapolists focus on man- made systems. Since dealing with natural systems involves "structural certainties" (trends based on the Laws of Nature), they place little, if any, faith in the ability of technology to "bail us out" of many of our problems. In fact, Negative Extrapolists believe that many of our problems are a result of a misguided application of technology.

Many of the works of Negative Extrapolists are issued as warnings much like primary forecasts: If we continue our present course of growth and maintain our "dominance over nature ethic," the ecological system will collapse and, with it, civilization as we now know it. Many writings of the Negative Extrapolists reflect a gloom and doom prospect for humankind. However, it is important to note that Margaret Mead (1970) in observing the need for such prophets said: "The role of the prophet of doom is a useful one only if it is not believed by the prophets themselves—the more vigorously Doomsday is preached, the more one is committed to a better world."

Negative Extrapolists believe:

—The pessimistic trendscited by this group are selected from "structural certainties," or Laws of Nature, which are fixed and constant, i.e. gravity on Earth.
—The current policyapproaches of governments will lead to doom.
—Technology causes more problems than it solves.
—Growth(economic, industrial)will lead to ecological disaster.
—Global equityis considered a central issue to be resolved.
—Discontinuous change and the collapse of civilization is inevitable if the future is left to "expert" decision makers.

Negative Extrapolists believe there are definite limits to our physical (environmental) systems, and that humankind is in a continuous state of error by increasing the pollution levels, depleting finite resource bases, and increasing stress on the ecological systems through population growth. They are saying that the current way of doing things will not work and that options are needed. The group which is best-known for generating options and alternatives is known as the Visionary School of Thought.

THE VISIONARIES or TRANSFORMATIONISTS

The second school of futurists is the Visionary School. Individuals who belong to this group are interested in generating new branches on the futures tree. Both the Positive and Negative Extrapolists look at past trends and then extrapolate the characteristics of those trends into the future. The work of the visionary is to offer alternatives. The visionary school offers optional or alternative ways of getting from a probable future (extrapolist in nature) to a more preferable future. Because of their style of work, visionaries tend to be concerned, but optimistic. Much of their work is concerned with modification of current values, environmental systems, and social institutions.

Even within the Visionary School of Thought, there are three distinct visions. However, certain shared assumptions exist. Most visionaries begin with a view similar to the Negative Extrapolists: "Something is definitely wrong and should be changed." From there, the sub-groups of visionaries go in very different directions. However, all are concerned with creating a new social order.

The **Environmental Visionaries** believe that the environment shapes both personal values and social institutions. They point to the low self-esteem of many individuals who live in the deprived conditions of certain urban environments. If the environment was changed for the better, they reason, then the values and institutions would also improve. The most fascinating work by environmental visionaries includes Gerald O'Neill's focus on space habitats and Jerome Glenn's descriptions of the prototypical communities: Arco-Santi and Auroville.

Environmental Visionaries believe:
— The best future can be realized by altering the physical environment (space/undersea colonies); new values and social inventions will follow.
— Current policyon reshaping the environment is considered too conservative.
— Technology is often considered good, as is economic growth.
— Global equity is a pressing issue.

The **Spiritual Visionaries'** argument is simple: The values widely held by humankind do not allow spiritual fulfillment. We are trapped and oppressed by our value structure and, as a result, the condition of humankind is increasingly unacceptable. The spiritual visionaries see many of our current crises as signs of hope, for they offer opportunities to introduce changes which will lead to a new age in which Humankind will rise above its materialistic pursuits to a higher, more spiritual state. Willis Harman and Marilyn Ferguson are leading spiritual visionaries.

Spiritual Visionaries believe:
— The best future can be created by altering the values of individuals; environment and social inventions will follow.
— Current policy are based on the wrong values.
— Technology is often considered bad, as is economic growth.
— Global equityis a pressing issue which must be resolved to promote global harmony.

The **Societal Visionaries** believe that both social institutions (such as public schools) and various levels of government serve to perpetuate old values and inhumane environments. If the social institutions were changed to allow more creativity and personal freedom, then people could pursue higher goals; and the result would be a better future. The value of technology rests on whether it will have a stabilizing or destabilizing effect on society. If a technology has a stabilizing effect on society, then it should be introduced. If the proposed technology has a destabilizing effect, then its ultimate value must be questioned. Works by Robert Theobald, Hazel Henderson, and Lester Brown are representative of this school of thought.

Societal Visionaries believe:
— The best future can be created by altering social institutions; values and the environment will follow.
— Current policy builds the wrong institutions.
— Technologyis sometimes considered bad, as is economic growth.
— Global equity is a major issue which must be resolved to induce more social harmony.

All visionary sub-groups hold certain indisputable points. All advocate a better, more preferable future. As your "futures" knowledge increases, you may be drawn to one of these sub-groups.

CLIENT-CENTERED FUTURISTS

Client-centered futurists help decision makers as they choose appropriate options and investigate the impacts of those options. Their task is to: 1) become familiar with the problem presented by their client, 2) generate possible solutions, and 3) aid the decision maker in making choices. Rarely do Client-centered futurists present only the final solution—that remains the task of the client. Client-entered futurists often work in think tanks and as private consultants.

Client-Centered Futurists believe:
—This group exists to aid decision makers in determining their choice of options.
—No particular image of the future is held beyond the basic premises of the field.
—An eclectic mix of methodologies is used.
—Data chosen tend to be local/from the client, extrapolist in nature, recent, and quantifiable.
—This group focuses on single issues instead of holistic systems.
—Bottom-line conclusions are rarely drawn; primarily options and impacts are presented for the client to act on.

When corporations need insight into future conditions, they hire Client-centered futurists as consultants. The main task is to tell the client what is probable on various horizons: how future events could affect the business effort of the client. Client-centered futurists are only responsible to their clients, not to the general welfare of the society or global community. Because their work is tailored to the needs of their clients, they do not have a group ideology, as with the visionaries. Since much of their work is done for corporations or government agencies, the results may be secret and the sole property of the client. The professional fields from which the client-centered futurists come are extremely diverse: Physics, engineering, urban planning, social science, management..., the list goes on. This diversity of backgrounds correlates directly to the diversity of the clients for whom this branch of futurists work.

As you can see, each school of thought is concerned with generating choices for our future. The different forecasts made by each school of thought represent values and assumptions from the broad continuum of possibilities that will ultimately become our future.

Whaley, C. (1984, second printing: 1986). *Future Studies: Personal and Global possibilities.* New York: Trillium Press.

Whaley, C., Whaley, H. (1986). *Future Images: Futures Studies for Grades 4-12.* New York: Trillium Press.

^^^

EVALUATION:

____ Good ____ Satisfactory ____ Unsatisfactory (explain)____ Satisfactory with modification

LIST MODIFICATIONS/EXPLANATIONS ON THE BACK

SUGGESTED GRADE LEVEL: All

ACTIVITY TITLE: *Carrying Capacities and the Eco-System*

GOALS INVOLVED: (1) (2)   3   (4)   ALL

CHARACTERISTICS OF FORESIGHT INVOLVED: (1)   (2)   3   (4)

GENERIC CONCEPTS INVOLVED: Population, Environment, Systems, Change, Interdependence, Technology.

OTHER NON-SPECIFIED OBJECTIVES: To better understand the nature of exponential growth and the impact of technology on the ability of our planet to support increased population.

ACTIVITIES/EXERCISES (facilitating goal accomplishment)

All populations tend to expand to fill their environment. "Natural Carrying Capacity," (N.C.C.) is the natural ability of a given area of land to support life. The area of land may range from a backyard to the entire planet. The life form which the area supports may range from the smallest organism in a desert to the densest rain forest. The natural carrying capacity of a given area then, is based upon many different factors: fertility and temperature of the soil, rainfall, the amount of solar income, and so on.

The natural carrying capacity of a given area determines what size of populations may inhabit that area. If the population(s) swells beyond the natural carrying capacity of its environment the population is in an "overshoot" condition. The population has overshot the environment's capacity to support it.

Once in an overshoot condition, there are only two options: immediate, controlled reduction of demand upon the environment through various means (good and bad), or go into "collapse" and let the environment purge itself of the excess population. Much of the suffering in certain parts of the world is a direct result of too many people in too small an area; the environment has become inadequate for the demands of the population: overshoot and collapse.

Technology may be used to increase or extend the carrying capacity of an area. The use of technology to elevate the natural carrying capacity of an area results in the term "extended, or Technological Carrying Capacity" (T.C.C.).

Two related examples would be the use of aquaducts in Rome to provide water for an expanding population, and the use of high technology to provide water for the growing population and farming efforts in the desert southwest. Examples of technology increasing an area's carrying capacity may be found in every major metropolitan area. A positive extrapolist would say: "See, because of technology we can have this many people here and now without straining the environment. A negative extrapolist would reply: "Since technology is man-made it is a 'subjective certainty' and as such, it could fail, creating a disasterous mistake."

Below is a simple graphic illustration of an overshoot and collapse series. The natural carrying capacity is shown as a dotted line. The extended carrying capacity is shown as a line of asterisks.

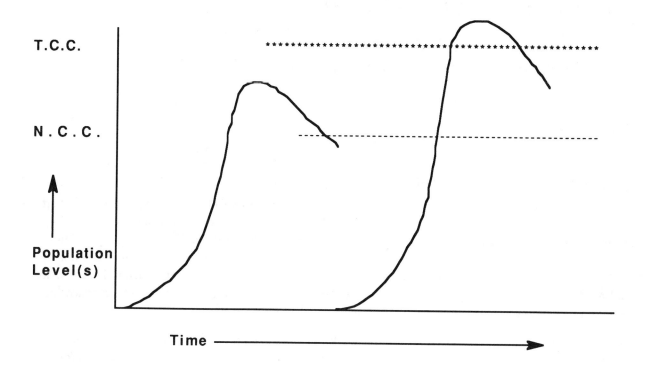

DISCUSSION QUESTIONS/ACTIVITIES:

Discuss the impact of technology on carrying capacity. Discuss the ramifications of a systems collapse should the technology fail.

Brainstorm possible problems springing from overpopulation then develop Futures Wheels based on:

#1 Overpopulation — determine the essentials needed to support a sustained, long-term increase in global population (ie. food, shelter, energy, air, water, eco-system, etc.)

#2 Technology — determine the necessary applications of technology to relieve stress on the "essentials" identified in #1.

RESOURCES USED:

Pirages, Dennis; *The New Context for International Relations: Global Eco-Politics*, Duxbury Press, Belmont, CA., 1978.

^^

EVALUATION:

____ Good ____ Satisfactory ____ Unsatisfactory (explain)____ Satisfactory with modification

LIST MODIFICATIONS/EXPLANATIONS ON THE BACK

SUGGESTED GRADE LEVEL: Upper Elementary -Middle School

ACTIVITY TITLE: *E.T. Life Confirmed?*

GOALS INVOLVED: 1   2   (3)   (4)   ALL

CHARACTERISTICS OF FORESIGHT INVOLVED: (1)   2   3   (4)   ALL

GENERIC CONCEPTS INVOLVED: Change, Conflict, Communication, Culture.

OTHER NON-SPECIFIED OBJECTIVES: To think about how much our civilization assumes "we are alone" and speculate on the possibility that we may have cosmic neighbors.

ACTIVITIES/EXERCISES (facilitating goal accomplishment)

Students awake to find a banner news headline: E.T. LIFE CONFIRMED? They read on to find that a team of archeologists and geologists found the skeleton of a probable extra-terrestial (possibly 3500-4000 years old) which was much like a human skeleton with the exceptions of slightly different joints, spine and size of cranium. The scientists found some type of equipment near the location of the skeleton. Upon analysis of the molecular composition of the equipment it was determined that it could not have been made on this planet: Earth has no metals or alloys like it. Although no spaceship was found, it's believed that the spaceship was made of the similar material.

ELEMENTARY: Draw a picture of what you think the E.T. looked like when it was alive. Discuss what your reaction would be, then discuss what reactions your parents, friends, and minister/ priest/rabbi might have.

Questions such as the following should be presented and discussed with students before they begin their work.

1.   What did the extra-terrestrial look like? How was it different from Earthlings?

2.   Where did it come from? Why did it decide to come to Earth?

3.   What language did it speak? How did it communicate with its own people? Do you think it communicated with Earthlings? If so, what did it tell them?

4.   What effect did this visit have on the Earthlings who met the extra-terrestrial? What were their reactions?

5.   Imagine that you were living when this alien being visited the planet Earth. Who were you? What did you think when you saw him? Using this point of view, write a story describing your encounter with this being.

After discussing these questions, students should be allowed to experiment with the resulting ideas. Follow-up projects could be in the form of a journal of an Earthling who met and interacted with the extra-terrestrial, a series of pictures depicting the alien's visit on earth, a scenario or story written from the alien's point of view, telling why and how he decides to visit this planet, or a play depicting the alien's visit and his interactions with people on Earth. Students should share the results of their work with the class, and the different points of view should be noted.

MIDDLE SCHOOL: Discuss what reactions the government, military, and religion would have. What might be their public positions on the discovery?

1. Assign three students the roles of mayor, minister, and chief of police of the town where the alien first made contact. Instruct students to consider the points of view their characters might have had. Stage a press conference with these individuals, with the rest of the class acting as the newspaper reporters assigned to cover the case. This activity could be expanded to include members of the community, parents and children.

2. What do you suppose the reactions would be of these people? Give reasons for your answer.

   — the Governor of the state where the alien landed,
   — the chief of police of the town where the alien landed,
   — a middle school student of this town,
   — the principal of the middle school,
   — the principal's wife,
   — the thermo-dynamics engineer at the local nuclear power plant,
   — YOU.

^^

EVALUATION:

____ Good ____ Satisfactory ____ Unsatisfactory (explain)____ Satisfactory with modification

LIST MODIFICATIONS/EXPLANATIONS ON THE BACK

SUGGESTED GRADE LEVEL:

ACTIVITY TITLE: *"Interdisciplinary Trash"*

GOALS INVOLVED: 1   2   3   4   (ALL)

CHARACTERISTICS OF FORESIGHT INVOLVED: 1   2   3   4   (ALL)

GENERIC CONCEPTS INVOLVED: Systems, interdependence, change, communication, culture/lifestyle, population, environment, technology.

OTHER NON-SPECIFIED OBJECTIVES: Develop a concern for environmental stewardship and the merits of recycling.

ACTIVITIES/EXERCISES (facilitating goal accomplishment)

SOLID WASTE FACTS

—Here are two definitions which may help you better understand the "SOLID WASTE FACTS."

> **SOLID WASTE:** a wide variety of discarded solid materials (and some contained liquids) including *rubbish* (Any collection of discarded wood-based products such as newspapers, wooden boxes, and cardboard), *trash* (similar to rubbish except it is not found in the home. It includes tree trimmings, lawn cuttings, bags of leaves, etc.), *garbage* (any animal or vegetable matter capable of decomposing, such as food wastes), and *bulky wastes*.

> **WASTE STREAM:** all the waste generated in the production, use, and disposal of goods. The total waste produced by a community or society, as goods move from origin to disposal.

—The average American tosses out between four to six pounds of solid waste per day, far more than our nearest competitors, the Europeans and Japanese. In just one year we toss out 144,000,000 TONS of solid waste. This is enough trash to make a road 16' wide and 1" thick from the Earth to the Moon..., every year!

Find the distances to the different planets. Then calculate how many years (at 144 tons of trash per year) it would take to build a "waste road" to the different planets?

At home set up a separate trash container (a large paper grocery bag) for different types of trash: one for paper, one for plastics, and one for aluminum. Make a graph showing how many bags of each type of trash your family generates in a day, a week, or a month. After the agreed upon time period for recording the information has past, create a graph with other members of the class showing how many bags the families of your entire class generated.

—Below are some facts about cities in various industrialized nations and their daily solid waste stream (in pounds per person):

New York City	4.0 lbs. per day
Hamburg, West Germany	1.9 lbs. per day
Paris, France	2.4 lbs. per day
Rome, Italy	1.5 lbs. per day
Tokyo, Japan	3.0 lbs. per day

Source: National Solid Wastes Management Association

Calculate how many pounds of waste each person creates in one year, ten years, thirteen years.

Make a bar graph showing the information on the above cities.

Find out how many people live in each of these major cities of the world and calculate the total waste generated by the population in one day.

—Sources say we could recycle two-thirds of the trash we currently throw-away. Recycling saves energy as well as natural resources. For example, it takes *20 times more energy to make new aluminum* from its source (bauxite) than it does to make recycled aluminum!

Make a list of some recyclable materials and products which we normally throw away. Into what products are these materials recycled?

—Recent studies show that about 640,000 plastic containers are discarded by the world's shipping fleet *every day.* Each year, fishing vessels reportedly dispose of about 52,000,000 pounds of plastic packaging material and lose more than 298,000,000 pounds of synthetic fishing gear, including nets, lines and buoys. More than 100,000 marine mammals and untold numbers of sea birds become entangled in this plastic debris.

—At least 50 species of sea birds and most sea turtles mistake floating plastic for food. A recent study of albatross chicks on Midway Island in the Pacific found that 9 out of 10 chicks had plastic in their gullets, apparently fed to them by the parents who had mistaken the plastic for prey.

—Beach litter is another serious dimension of the waste and litter problem. On a single day in September 1988, a Texas beach cleanup sponsored by the Center for Marine Conservation (formerly the Center for Environmental Education) brought in more than one ton of litter per mile of beach! Most of the debris had been discarded at sea from vessels and oil rigs. The booty contained:

48,197	bottles,
31,773	bags,
15,631	plastic six-pack holders,
4,225	fishing lines,
1,914	diapers,
1,719	fishing nets,
930	syringes, and
225	hard hats.

Source: Waste Management Inc., January 1988 WMI Report

Make a circle or bar graph showing the above information in a graph form.

********* SAVE VALUABLE RESOURCES for YOUR FUTURE*********

—Recycling saves 65%-95% of the ENERGY needed to produce NEW cans.

—17 trees are saved from each ton of recycled newspaper.

—9 gallons of oil is saved for every ton of recycled glass.

—What is the U.S. solid waste stream composed of?

Paper, cardboard	35.6%
Yard waste	20.1%
Food waste	8.9%
Metals	8.9%
Glass	8.4%
Plastics	7.3%
Wood	4.1%
Rubber, leather	2.8%
Cloth	2.0%
Other	1.9%
TOTAL	100.0%

Source: Environmental Protection Agency

Why are some items such a high percentage and other items so low?

Make a circle or bar graph showing the above information.

********************* JUNK MAIL FACTS *************************

Americans receive 2 million TONS of junk mail each year

—44% is never opened or read,

—Junk mail uses 100 million trees annually,

—One day's worth could heat 250,000 American homes,

—People spend eight months of their entire lives dealing with junk mail.

To help somebody get OFF the junk mail list, have them write to:

Mail Preference Service

Direct Marketing Association

11 West 42nd Street

PO Box 3861

New York, NY 10163-3861

$$$$$$$$$$$$$$$$$$$$$$$$$$ TRASH COSTS $$$$$$$$$$$$$$$$$$$$$$$$$$$

—Americans spend $4,000,000,000 (That's four BILLION) each year just to collect, transport and dispose of trash.

List other projects and causes Americans could use that money for (i.e. hospitals, the homeless, education, crime, etc.).

—Under certain conditions, some organic waste can produce energy. Americans throw away enough organic waste to produce the energy equivalent of 80 million barrels of oil a year. That's $2.2 BILLION dollars worth—enough to provide the entire U.S. energy needs for four days!

—The U.S. wastes 1% of its total energy budget on throw-away beverage containers. Using recyclables could cut that figure in half.

—Americans spend almost 10% of their grocery bill on packaging which they then discard.

—Two-thirds of the annual paper production in the U.S. ends up in the trash. We don't know exactly how many trees that figure represents, but we do know there is a limited number of trees available at any given time.

Survey a grocery store for items which have excessive and/or elaborate packaging. After you have several items, determine some packaging alternatives which could be just as effective, or ask yourself the question; "Is any packaging really necessary for this item"? Just for fun, start in the produce section.

—Our national "balance of payments" represents how much money foreign countries pay us for U.S. goods versus how much money we pay foreign countries for their goods. It is generally a good idea to have foreign countries buy more goods from us than we buy from them. One way we could help our balance of payments would be to consider the following information:

"The U.S. imports 91% of its aluminum from foreign countries. We then throw most (over 1 million tons each year) of it away. An interesting question would be: From which countries do we get most of our aluminum? Or another point of view would be: to which countries do we send our dollars for a resource which we then throw away?"

Source: "The World's Trashiest People," *The Futurist,* 1981.

—Some day, asphalt highways may contain compounds made from old automobile tires. Until recently, tires have been very difficult to recycle. But, scientists have found that when rubber is frozen at very low temperatures, it shatters into a powder that can be used to make new roads. Experiments mixing very small pieces of shredded tires with asphalt are also now under way.

Source: *The Kids' Whole Catalog to the Future*

RECYCLING WALK: Take a walk around the school grounds or your neighborhood with a friend to identify and list the different types of litter you find. Then separate the list into recyclable or non-recyclable litter. Next, make a graph showing the results of your catagorizing and compare graphs with your classmates who have also taken a "recycling walk."

********************* **EARTH TO EARTH** *********************

From the moment a raw material is extracted from the earth by mining processes, until it is returned to the earth in a landfill, energy is constantly adding to its value. Below are all the major points where energy is used in the life and death of a product. Every time energy is added it becomes a part of the "hidden costs" for which we all pay for when we buy something. If the produce is reused or recycled those hidden costs GO WAY DOWN!

RAW MATERIALS ⟶ FACTORY, MFG ⟶ FINISHED PRODUCT ⟶
⟶ MARKET ⟶ HOME/USE ⟶ TRASH ⟶ LANDFILL.

Set up recycling stations around school for aluminum cans. You could make posters encouraging others to use the containers. Take the cans into an aluminum recycling facility and use the money for a class project at the end of the school year.

Make a collage about waste using newspaper clippings, cartoons, pictures, etc. As a class, collect information from newspapers and magazines about waste and/or recycling and create a bulletin board. You could also create your own cartoon about waste management issues.

** REBUILD THE U.S. AIRLINE FLEET EVERY THREE MONTHS!**

The Conservation and Renewable Energy Inquiry and Referral Service indicates that over half of the cities in the U.S. are running out of landfill space. Examples of the problem include:

— 16 billion disposable diapers are added to landfills every year,

— Enough aluminum is thrown away every 3 months to rebuild our ENTIRE airline fleet,

— The average city of 100,000 spends as much on trash disposal as they do on their police force.

To learn more about this problem write:

CAREIRS

P.O. Box 8900

Silver Springs, MD   20907

Ask for FS 150; "Municipal Resource Recovery," and/or FS 227; "Recycling Waste to Save Energy." These fact sheets are free and contain information not easily available from other sources.

The information in this activity is from: *Recycle Florida: A Curriculum Unit on the Merits of Recycling and Environmental Stewardship,* Leon County Schools, Tallahassee, FL., C. Whaley, Recycle Florida Curriculum Coordinator, 1989.

^^^

EVALUATION:

____ Good ____ Satisfactory ____ Unsatisfactory (explain)____ Satisfactory with modification

LIST MODIFICATIONS/EXPLANATIONS ON THE BACK

SUGGESTED GRADE LEVEL: Upper Elementary -Middle School

ACTIVITY TITLE: *Take Out The Trash!*

GOALS INVOLVED: 1   2   3   4   (ALL)

CHARACTERISTICS OF FORESIGHT INVOLVED: 1   2   3   4   (ALL)

GENERIC CONCEPTS INVOLVED: Systems, interdependence, change, communication, culture/lifestyle, population, environment, technology.

OTHER NON-SPECIFIED OBJECTIVES: Develop a concern for environmental stewardship and the merits of recycling.

ACTIVITIES/EXERCISES (facilitating goal accomplishment)

Long after we take out the trash, the contents of the garbage bag are still with us. Even though we throw things away, they don't instantly GO away. Some normal, everyday waste stays with us for as long as 1,000,000 years. The following are approximate times for decomposition of various items.

Cotton towel/rag	1-5 months
Rope	3-14 months
Wool sock	1 year
Bamboo pole	1-3 years
Painted wooden stake	13 years
Tin cans	100 years
Aluminum cans	200-500 years
Glass bottles	as much as 1 million years

Source: Wallace, I., Wallechinsky, D., et.al.; *Book of Lists 2,* William Morrow, N.Y., 1980.

On a sheet of paper, make a graph that will allow you to compare the different decomposition times for all items.

************* SOLID WASTE DISPOSAL OPTIONS*************

There are five ways to deal with solid waste:

1) **BURY IT:** in sanitary landfills

2) **BURN IT:** some waste is burned in incinerators. Some incinerators are built to channel the heat from the flames to boil water. The steam from the boiling water turns turbines which generate electricity which is then used in your community. This is known as "energy recovery." The type of facility which operates this way is called a "waste-to-energy," or W-T-E plant.

3) **REUSE IT:** to use something again for its original or other purpose. If an item cannot be recycled maybe it can be reused. Old clothes, furniture, and any number of other items can be given to individuals or agencies who then reuse or distribute items for reuse. Some items can be handy if reused around the home. Examples could be shopping bags and other items reused for the original or a different purpose. 4) RECYCLE IT: separating specific materials from other wastes and processing them so they may be used again.

5) **REDUCE IT:** simply reduce the need for items which are disposable or which have obvious built-in obsolescence. This choice may become the most important of all.

—How does the U.S. dispose of its solid waste?

> Landfill 80%
>
> Incinerated 10%
>
> Recycled 10%
>
> TOTAL 100%

Source: Environmental Protection Agency

What are the advantages and disadvantages of each of the above disposal methods?

Why do you suppose we depend on landfills so heavily in the U.S.? Are landfills easier or cheaper than the other choices?

With land values increasing in the future, do you think we will change our ways?

If we do change, what optional disposal method should we change to? Why?

Conduct a "recycling survey" of people in your community and report your results back to class. Some starter questions could be: What one thing could you change at home that would help a recycling effort? Do you think Americans are the "trashiest" people in the world? Would you be willing to use glasses instead of paper or styrofoam cups to help reduce our trash stream? etc.

—The following figures show the results of a statewide program called "Recycle America." This program has been instaued by Waste Management Inc., a waste collection and recycling firm in Florida. In one year alone, different divisions of the "Recycle America" program in Florida collected the following materials for recycling:

10,777	tons of corrugated paper
2,318	tons of paper (primarily newspaper)
168	tons of glass
192	tons of steel cans
26.5	tons of aluminum cans
14	tons of plastic

TOTAL: 13,495.50 TONS of recyclable material in just one year.

Make a bar graph and a circle graph of the above information. Which type of graph shows the information the most dramatically? Why?

^^

EVALUATION:

____ Good ____ Satisfactory ____ Unsatisfactory (explain)____ Satisfactory with modification

LIST MODIFICATIONS/EXPLANATIONS ON THE BACK

SUGGESTED GRADE LEVEL: Upper Elementary -Middle School

ACTIVITY TITLE: *"2030 A.D. The Recycling Rebound"*
(Introduction & Section A)

GOALS INVOLVED: 1 2 3 4 (ALL)

CHARACTERISTICS OF FORESIGHT INVOLVED: 1 2 3 4 (ALL)

GENERIC CONCEPTS INVOLVED: (All) Systems, interdependence, change, conflict, communication, culture, population, human dignity, technology, and environment.

ACTIVITIES/EXERCISES (facilitating goal accomplishment)

"2030 A.D.: The Recycling Rebound" is an extensive scenario which is from: *Recycle Florida: A Curriculum Unit on the Merits of Recycling and Environmental Stewardship*, Leon County Schools, Tallahassee, FL., C. Whaley, Recycle Florida Curriculum Coordinator, 1989. It contains three different sections: "The Road to Trouble," "Our Past Comes Back to Haunt Us," and The Big Turnaround." Each section has its own vocabulary words and specific questions designed to amplify certain concerns found in the section.

"2030 A.D.: THE RECYCLING REBOUND"

INTRODUCTION

"2030 A.D.: THE RECYCLING REBOUND" depicts a possible future state of affairs in which, through waste and apathy, we bring ourselves to the brink of economic collapse. The causes of this situation were many and the efforts to plan ahead were few. However, every element in the scenario is based on a simple extrapolation of actual current trends. "2030 A.D." is also designed to show the participant how the grim situation portrayed could be reversed in one generation.

As American manufacturing shifted into high gear many bad habits regarding use of natural resources and energy were born. Some wasteful practices which emerged in the period from 1920-1990 are examined in 2030 A.D. Americans finally realized they were literally throwing away their future. By simply changing their attitude regarding resources and energy usage, a negative economic situation could be reversed.

An optimistic ending develops to show students that through concerted action, people can exercise a greater degree of control over their future. Americans adopted a different frame of mind concerning our resources and energy: "Instead of treating natural resources like something we inherited from our rich uncle, we started treating them like something we were borrowing from a future generation."

SECTION A: "THE ROAD TO TROUBLE"
KEY VOCABULARY WORDS

SCENARIO: a story which describes a future situation or state of affairs.

EXTRAPOLATION: a simple linear projection of a known trend into the future.

APATHY: a lack of caring about something or someone.

FUTURIST: one who studies possible futures.

INFRARED: an invisible light lying outside the visable light spectrum and capable of photographing through darkness, haze, etc.

SUBTERRANEAN: below the surface of the earth.

SYNTHETIC: composed of artificial elements or parts, not made of natural components.

READING QUESTIONS FOR SECTION A

1) When does this story happen? In what ways have things changed since today?

2) What are "domes" and why do you think they exist?

3) What does the narrator imply about living outside the domes?

4) What is built-in obsolescence and how did it start?

5) What is "embodied energy"? Why do few people know of it? What role did it play in changing peoples attitudes toward energy use?

6) What did people think of recycling in the 1960's, 70's, and 80's?

7) Who, or what, was "OPEC" and what was its role in energy use?

SECTION A: "THE ROAD TO TROUBLE"

Looking out across the lush landscape inside Dome 18-B, it's hard to believe that at one time our nation—in fact, our world—was seriously threatened. The threat was not from enemy missiles or foreign terrorists, but from our own behavior and way of life. Most agree that our lifestyle was simply wasteful. We were our own worst enemy. Signs of that time period still exist outside our domes. Looking at the screen on the environmental scanner, I can still see underground areas of decay through the infrared filter. These subterranean areas of decay are remaining traces from the "Time of Trash" which lasted from about 1920 to a little past 2000.

The random dumping of wastes and other destructive behavior began in a distant past known as the "Industrial Age." During this time period, it appeared that many natural resources in the U.S. would last forever. Iron ore, copper, manganese, tungsten, lead, and many other minerals needed by industry were readily available from the Great Lakes and the Western mountain ranges. The softwood and hardwood forests of the South and Northwest supplied enormous amounts of wood for paper and other products. We were a nation rich with raw materials.

Because of our seeming wealth of resources, we produced and consumed products as if the supply would never end. We used materials and then threw them away. Energy was cheap, raw materials were abundant, and there were far fewer people to compete for the resources. The United States developed a wasteful attitude which lasted for decades. We became a "throw-away" society. We developed a "disposable product" mentality. We didn't know any better; after all, we **were** the land of plenty.

There were many reasons why we started making so many disposable products. One example can be found in the old automobile business. In the early days of the auto industry, a manufacturing strategy called built-in obsolescence contributed to our throw-away mentality. Built-in obsolescence was the planning and manufacturing of a product which was designed to last only a short length of time. In the beginning of car manufacturing, Henry Ford and his employees worked year after year making only those changes which increased the durability and improved the performance of the Model T. A competitor of Ford's, after falling behind in auto sales, decided to make yearly style changes which would make the new model appear more desirable and fashionable. Each year there were new features; new reasons to get rid of your old car and buy a new one. Mr. Ford decided to do the same and built-in obsolescence was born.

The auto industry was not the only industry with built-in obsolescence. Another example was the clothing industry which, was by definition, fashion-conscious. By producing new colors, materials, and styles each year, clothing designers caused several million "outdated" garments to be moth-balled annually. A major problem is that several million dollars worth of natural and synthetic fibers and the energy needed to retrieve, process, and manufacture the garments was moth-balled also.

Convenience also played a role in maintaining our throw-away society. It was so easy to come home, put a prepared dinner in the microwave, and eat 7-10 minutes later. Often, it was even a good meal. But what do you think happened to the paper packaging, aluminum foil, plastic plate, and energy it took to create these wrappings that came with the dinner? What about the several million other microwave-dinner-eaters that evening? What do you suppose happened to their microwave "trash?" Actual historical records show that even back in 1985, for every $100 Americans spent on groceries, $10 was for packaging which was then thrown out! Because of our wealth and consumption habits, many products, and the containers in which they came, were destined for the garbage heap. Materials such as metal, glass, and paper were usually thrown away after a single use. It became a way of life; after we were finished with something we would throw it away. The problem was we would THROW it away, but it wouldn't GO away. "America the Beautiful" had serious trash problems.

People in elementary and high school in the mid-eighties and ninties, but they can still remember how the environment looked and how much was wasted. Trash littered our parks and yards; it was tossed out of car windows to litter our streets and highways. Some trash was left in open dumps where it smelled, looked ugly, and attracted rats and other vermin. Some individuals and businesses burned trash in open fires on their property which polluted the air. Many people can even remember reading about waste being dumped into the oceans, only to wash back up on the shoreline, like a boomerang. Many Americans became used to our environment looking like trash, and they didn't think about the energy that was being thrown away simultaneously.

Most Americans didn't realize then that when they threw away materials after one usage, they wasted not only the material, but the energy it took to bring it to market. That was money we may as well have just given to the Organization of Petroleum Exporting Countries, or OPEC for short. If we had known how much we were going to need that money for other uses at home in the U.S. we might have changed our ways. Now we know that every time we buy something, we are also buying a certain amount of valuable "embodied energy." Embodied energy is the energy it took to mine and transport the raw materials, get the workers to the factory, actually make the product, distribute the product to the market, advertise it, and of course, the energy it took you to get the product home. If the material is used twice, the energy cost needed to manufacture is not as great. If the product is re-used several times, through a recycling process, costs go way down.

Even as late as the early 1990's, many people still considered recycling messy, complicated, uneconomical, and unnecessary in many parts of the country. Little did we realize that recycling would eventually be required by law in some states and violators would be handed stiff jail terms.

SUGGESTED GRADE LEVEL: Upper Elementary -High School

ACTIVITY TITLE: *"2030 A.D. The Recycling Rebound" (Section B)*

GOALS INVOLVED: 1   2   3   4   (ALL)

CHARACTERISTICS OF FORESIGHT INVOLVED: 1   2   3   4   (ALL)

GENERIC CONCEPTS INVOLVED: All

ACTIVITIES/EXERCISES (facilitating goal accomplishment)

"2030 A.D.: The Recycling Rebound" is an extensive scenario which is from: *Recycle Florida: A Curriculum Unit on the Merits of Recycling and Environmental Stewardship*, Leon County Schools, Tallahassee, FL, 1989.

SECTION B: "OUR PAST COMES BACK TO HAUNT US"

SECTION B: KEY VOCABULARY WORDS

ETHIC: a system of behavior reflecting a person's values.

STEWARDSHIP: the responsibility of an individual toward goods or objects entrusted to his care.

READING QUESTIONS FOR SECTION B

1) How did gasoline prices rise to $6.22 a gallon? How did that affect driving in the mid to late 1990's?

2) What percentage of the annual paper production in the 1980's ended up in the trash?

3) What is the basis for "hidden costs"? In how many ways did hidden costs affect us?

4) What role did manufacturers play in the hidden costs problem? What role did consumers play?

5) What is the connection between how much is wasted, how much it costs, and how long raw materials last in the future?

6) How does waste affect your future? Will it affect you more than people who are older than you or younger than you?

7) What is bauxite? About how much aluminum do we now throw-away? What does the following statement mean: "The question was: From which countries do we get most of our aluminum, OR, in other words, To which countries do we send our dollars for a resource which we then throw away?

8) What is the connection between problems, inaction, and loss of possible solutions?

SECTION B: "OUR PAST COMES BACK TO HAUNT US"

In the 1970s, international oil shortages sent shock waves through the industrialized world. America was not spared. Almost overnight, the fuel needed for heating, manufacturing, operating vehicles, and making different types of products like detergents, nylon, plastics, and substances for making vinyl and cosmetics, suddenly wasn't there. Lines of cars stretched for blocks at gas stations. Behind the scenes, governmental agencies quietly started shifting energy away from some uses to other needs for reasons of national security.

Because of an increasing shortage of resources and a second series of energy shortages in the late 1990's, gasoline eventually went to $6.22 a gallon in the spring of 1999. Prices soared on some products and rose slowly on most other items. Anything which needed oil for production— from plastic wrap, to paint, to lawn fertilizer—became unaffordable for more and more people. Because of their skyrocketing prices and the cost of fuel, cars were owned by groups of people instead of individuals. They were rarely driven unless they were packed with people. Buildings were never heated above 60 degrees and air conditioning was nearly a thing of the past.

Beverages were sold in bulk because the energy needed to mine and manufacture the aluminum was being diverted to other, "more important national security needs." Plastic containers, popular in the 70's and 80's, were not available because of the oil needed to manufacture the container, not to mention the oil needed to run the factories and transport products to market. People refilled old containers or they simply did without.

Eventually, paper became scarce. The energy available to plant, raise, cut the trees, then process them to pulp and finally into paper, was slowly shifted to other, more pressing needs. Paper became another victim of priorities. Over time the daily newspaper, stationery and paper for school and business was increasingly rare. When it was available, few people could afford the luxury. With shame, many people remembered the 80s when two-thirds of the annual U.S. paper production ended in the trash. It is difficult to know how many trees that figure represented. It seemed no one cared that only a limited number of mature trees still existed.

We finally started to realize we had been throwing away our future! This would be particularly true for the younger generation. The youth were the ones that would inherit the serious shortages and the major problems associated with long-term wastefulness. Our "out of sight, out of mind" mentality was sending us to the poor house. There was a stirring among the young, who saw themselves being sold down the river because of the waste. The youth organized. They came to realize that waste has "hidden costs." Because so much more is produced than is needed, more is thrown away. America's economic problems arose because of wasted energy, pollution, and wasted raw materials; all a result of overproduction. And if that wasn't enough, more money was needed for waste collection, disposal, and buying land for landfills.

One last hidden cost involved America's foreign trade deficit. The U.S. kept spending its dollars in foreign countries to buy raw materials which we were then wasting! There was a definite connection between how much we wasted, how much it cost, and how long the raw materials would last in the future. Products ranging from paper plates, plasticware, and razors, to lighters, flashlights, and paint rollers, were sold as "throw-away" products.

Every day, millions of people ate in cafeterias and restaurants in which napkins, plates, salt, pepper, salad dressing, butter, styrofoam, and more were simply thrown away. These items required energy, raw materials, and manufacturing time, and all these items were representative of American overproduction. Because the hidden costs were difficult to notice, we didn't realize the long-range implications of our actions. Now we do. Manufacturers must take part of the blame for producing and packaging products in a "disposable" way. Consumers must take the rest of the blame for using so many disposable items. Once the U.S. was second only to the Soviet Union in non-fuel minerals. However, because our consumption levels have been so great since the 1920's, we have become importers of many of these minerals. Bauxite, from which aluminum is made, is a good example. Historical records show in the mid 1980's, the U.S. was importing 91% of its bauxite. In the same time period, Americans were throwing out most (over 1 million tons per year) of that imported aluminum after only one use. The question became: From which countries do we get most of our aluminum, OR, in other words, to which countries do we send our dollars for a resource which we then throw away?

Our energy and natural resource shortages required the U.S. to re-evaluate its resource policies and try to reverse the damage caused by our throw-away mentality. If we were to survive and keep ourselves from becoming a poor nation, we would have to use our resources and energy in a better way for the future. Most Americans began to feel: "What's gone is gone; there isn't much to be done about that now. BUT, what we can we do to assure we take care of what's left?"

Looking back, the beginnings of our "Time of Trash" era becomes clear: the resource and energy shortage began as an issue which needed some attention by individuals or government or both. We continued to throw away energy and resources until the issue became a problem. Because of our continued inaction during "warning situations," such as the energy shortage era of the 70's, several different solutions were lost to us. The remaining choices available to us were more drastic and costly. In the meantime, the amount of trash kept piling up.

Just as the issue had been allowed to grow into a major problem, the problem was compounded by further inaction until the problem became a crisis. As we now fully realize, the longer we wait to solve any problem, the greater the risks and the fewer the choices available to us.

SUGGESTED GRADE LEVEL: Upper Elementary -High School

ACTIVITY TITLE: *2030 A.D. The Recycling Rebound (Section C)*

GOALS INVOLVED: 1   2   3   4   (ALL)

CHARACTERISTICS OF FORESIGHT INVOLVED: 1   2   3   4   (ALL)

GENERIC CONCEPTS INVOLVED: All

ACTIVITIES/EXERCISES (facilitating goal accomplishment)

"2030 A.D.: The Recycling Rebound" is an extensive scenario which is from: *Recycle Florida: A Curriculum Unit on the Merits of Recycling and Environmental Stewardship,* Leon County Schools, Tallahassee, FL., 1989. It contains three different sections: "The Road to Trouble," "Our Past Comes Back to Haunt Us," and "The Big Turnaround." Each section has its own vocabulary words and specific questions designed to amplify certain concerns from the section.

SECTION C: "THE BIG TURNAROUND"

SECTION C: KEY VOCABULARY WORDS

WANTON: lacking discipline, not susceptable to control; given to self-indulgence and the enjoyment of luxury.

FINITE: having limits.

FRUGAL, FRUGALITY: economical, thrifty.

BOYCOTT: to refuse to buy goods from, or trade with, a particular business.

READING QUESTIONS FOR SECTION C:

1) Explain the shift in attitude reflected in the following statement: "Instead of treating natural resources like something we inherited from our rich uncle, we started treating them like something we were borrowing from a future generation."

2) How were long lasting products different from the "throw-away" products? Did they cost more or less than the throw-away products?

3) What kinds of lifestyle changes did people have to make for the "new conservation ethic?"

4) What role did young people play in turning our wasteful society around? Why were they so concerned?

SECTION C: "THE BIG TURNAROUND"

Some time between the years 1925 and 2000, our global resource situation had changed for the worse. The amount of natural resources and non-renewable sources of energy had decreased. This change for the worse had been subtle, almost unnoticed by most people over the seventy-five year period. The change was now irreversible and demanded careful use of, and concern for, our remaining resources. The days of wanton waste were over. Instead of treating natural resources like something we inherited from a rich uncle, we started treating them like something we were borrowing from a future generation. Resources became something to be taken care of and shared with future generations. The younger generation was starting to demand it! Changing resource levels and increasing pressure from young people continues to save us from becoming an energy- and resource-starved nation and world.

In the mid 1990s, an organization of youth known as W.A.S.T.E. (War Against Senseless Trashing of the Environment) suggested humankind was given Spaceship Earth for a better reason than to wreck it with pollution. W.A.S.T.E. strongly encouraged local, state, and national government action which, in time, would allow sensible and environmentally sound practices to evolve.

The wasteful behavior of industrialized nations in the latter half of the twentieth century gave way to the realization that we had a planet with finite resources which called for wise management. American maufacturers started building products that would last! High design quality, durability, and efficient use of energy became top priorities. Prices didn't go down as some had hoped, but since the products did last longer, they were actually cheaper in the long run.

Those individuals and companies who didn't adopt conservation measures and create recyclable products were often boycotted by W.A.S.T.E. and another, more militant group known as T.R.A.S.H. (Teens Rally Against Senseless Habits). W.A.S.T.E., T.R.A.S.H., and other groups in the U.S. and abroad, would boycott wasteful companies until the companies eventually went out of business or changed their ways. The days of "built-in obsolescence" and intentional manufacturing of "disposable products" became a shameful memory.

National, state, and local contests, in which children and adults were encouraged to come up with creative ideas for saving energy and natural resources, flourished. Ideas were as simple as reusing paper grocery bags instead of plastic bags as wastepaper basket liners or creating compost piles rather than bagging grass cuttings and leaves. Individual ideas for creating new recyclable products were also suggested and put into practice.

At first, our conservation and stewardship measures seemed like a major inconvenience, even a sacrifice. However, as time passed, more people realized that we had consumed so much for so long we couldn't continue at that same level of consumption. In our cutback, we developed a fun- house mirror view of our old selves: swollen in the middle from our past excesses. We were trimming down, recycling, and finding ways to live better.

Over time, we realized that this new conservation ethic did not mean a lower quality of life. It meant living in a different way. We would have to change our ways from extravagance to conservation, from inefficiency to frugality.

By recycling much of our "trash," our economy was growing stronger. We were sending far fewer dollars to foreign countries for oil and mineral resources which we had wasted and thrown away in the past. Since we were using energy and raw materials more sensibly, pollution levels slowly but surely started to decline. We were beginning to see a cleaner, safer environment and a much brighter future. All the "hidden costs" of which we had been unaware earlier, or had simply ignored, became more apparent. Led by the young people, and through personal and collective efforts, we had avoided the disaster borne of our waste and lack of concern for the future.

UNIT SURVEY: DISCUSSION QUESTIONS

The following questions are designed to elicit higher-order thinking than the reading questions at the beginning of Parts A, B, and C.

1) Why did it take so long before America saw the massive problem made by waste?

2) How did the fashion industry contribute to the "Trashing of America"? Make a list of other possible contributing industries and discuss the effects of each.

3) What is the relationship between the energy needed to produce something and "hidden costs" mentioned in the scenario?

4) Discuss convenience products and practices in the "throw-away society." What were the resulting problems and how did it all start?

5) What were the arguments used against recycling in the 1980's and early '90's? Why did those arguments succeed for so long?

6) Which industries and what products mentioned in the scenario depended on oil? What others industries can you think of? What would be the results if suddenly we did not have the oil?

7) Besides those mentioned in the scenario, what popular paper products do you think added to the destruction of the country's forests?

8) What is meant by the phrase, "out of sight, out of mind mentality"?

9) What is "stewardship" and how does it apply to our environment?

10) What are some examples of unnecessary and wasteful packaging of products?

11) As the level of consumption was reduced, the need for imported raw materials decreased. What might have been some effects of our reduced spending for raw materials on the people of foreign nations such as Surinam and the Philippines?

12) Explain the relationship between: a) raw materials usage, b) over-production of goods, and c) energy usage/waste. How could this combination make a wealthy nation like the U.S. poor?

13) The production of long-lasting products meant fewer products needed to be manufactured. Discuss the effects this could have on society (jobs, standard of living, etc.) What solutions can you generate to overcome the negative effects on our society?

14) Why did the youth of the country become so involved? Can you think of other times in history when the young people of a country were the catalyst for change? If you were to join one group or the other (W.A.S.T.E. or T.R.A.S.H.) which would you join and why?

^^^

EVALUATION:

____ Good ____ Satisfactory ____ Unsatisfactory (explain)____ Satisfactory with modification

LIST MODIFICATIONS/EXPLANATIONS ON THE BACK

SUGGESTED GRADE LEVEL: Upper Elementary -Middle School

ACTIVITY TITLE: *Simulation: "Not in My Backyard"*

GOALS INVOLVED: (1) (2) 3 (4) ALL

CHARACTERISTICS OF FORESIGHT INVOLVED: (1) (2) 3 (4) ALL

GENERIC CONCEPTS INVOLVED: Systems, interdependence, change, conflict, communication, population, environment.

OTHER NON-SPECIFIED OBJECTIVES: To better understand the size of the solid waste problem in this country and its implications for the future.

ACTIVITIES/EXERCISES (facilitating goal accomplishment)

SIMULATION: "NOT IN MY BACKYARD"

Background Information

Like most other towns in Florida, Smithson Center's population is growing in leaps and bounds. More buildings have gone up to accommodate increasing numbers of businesses and homeowners. The economy in the past has been very strong although there are signs of growing problems, economic and otherwise.

One problem with the increasing numbers has been the amount of waste generated. Not only has there been more of the normal household wastes but also waste from increased construction and businesses. Clearly Smithson Center's waste stream has grown radically.

The projected life of the two current landfills will expire in five years. They were intended to last longer but when the landfills were first planned and built no one foresaw the high degree of population increase.

What to do with Smithson Center's increasing volume of waste is becoming a heated issue. The City-County Council recognizes the need for new disposal facilities, and soon! The problem is that no one wants a landfill, incinerator, or any other type of disposal "in their backyard." In addition, shipping the waste to a neighboring county's sanitary landfill would be very costly. Besides, they're in the same situation: they are in a high growth mode and don't need anyone else's waste!

The prospect of increasing waste disposal costs, besides the general increase in taxes to handle the growth, does not sit well with most of the population. The heightened emotions due to increasing costs pale in significance when compared to what happens when the council proposes a new site for the new landfill. An activist group, S.L.O.P. (Stop Landfills Or Perish), is advocating no new landfills and threatening the politicians with removal from office (i.e., "Perish"). Unfortunately, they are not suggesting any alternative solutions.

Using the information from Futures Activities #25-29, local resources (i.e. recycling agencies, local landfill operators, etc.), and your problem-solving abilities, you will play a role in solving Smithson Center waste problems.

On a separate sheet of paper, analyze and describe your position as though you were:

a) the Mayor

b) (one of) six City-County Council members (include your position as representative from a proposed landfill site)

c) three representatives of the S.L.O.P. membership

d) a local landfill owner/operator

e) the head of the City-County Planning Agency

f) the owners of major construction companies

g) the owners of a group of local restaurants

h) a group of private (trash) haulers

i) the owners of a large number of apartment buildings

j) two entreprenuers who want to start a recycling center business

k) a broadcast media team who have been covering this issue

DIRECTIONS: There will be a town council meeting in the classroom and all the above players will attend and present their point of view. After analyzing each position, the players will either choose, or be assigned to, a particular role. Players will advocate their position as though they were that individual with his or her interests in mind. Since the players have analyzed everyone's position they will have a better idea of where they are coming from and be in a much better position to make their argument more persuasive during the council meeting.

Determine the answers to the following questions. The answers will be helpful in the above roles.

— On the average, how much total daily waste does Smithson Center produce if its population is similar to your community? (Call local landfills and approximate a figure.)

— What would be the best method, or combination of methods, to solve the waste problem? (options: recycle, reuse, reduce, burn for energy, landfill.)

— Based on the information in the field, about what percentage of Smithson Center's waste could be recycled?

— In what ways could you insure that the community will agree with, and take part in, a recycling effort? What organizations could you call on to help?

SIMULATION GOALS

—To propose actions for properly and safely disposing of Smithson Center's growing waste stream.

—To weigh the short-and long-term consequences of each proposal.

—To reach consensus on which final plan of action to implement.

GROUP RULES FOR THE SIMULATION

—Class ground rule: no personal criticism.

—There should be a recorder and spokesperson for each group.

—Put yourself in your character's role (consider their business and/or group objectives, etc.).

—Students may not interrupt a speaker who has the floor. Potential speakers must be recognized by the moderator (teacher or designee).

^^^

EVALUATION:

____ Good ____ Satisfactory ____ Unsatisfactory (explain)____ Satisfactory with modification

LIST MODIFICATIONS/EXPLANATIONS ON THE BACK

REFERENCES

Coates, J. & Jarratt, J. (1990). What futurists believe. *The Futurist;* Bethesda, MD: World Future Society, Vol. 24, #6, November/December.

Dewey, J. (1902). *The School in Society.* London: University of Chicago Press, Ltd.

Fowles, J. (ed.). (1978). *Handbook of Futures Research.* Westport, CT: Greenwood Press.

The Futurist; (1988) "Future Scope" Section. Bethesda, MD: World Future Society, Vol.22, #3, May/June, p. 5.

George, P. & Gallagher, J. (1978). Children's thoughts about the future: A comparison of gifted and non-gifted students. *Journal for the education of the gifted,* 2 (1), p. 33-42.

Gallagher, J. (1985). *Teaching the gifted child.* Boston: Allyn and Bacon.

Hawken, P., Ogilvy, J., Schwartz, P. (1982). *Seven tomorrows.* New York: Bantam Books.

Johnson, Lynell (1987). Children's vision of the future, *The Futurist,* Bethesda, MD: World Future Society, May/June p. 39.

Jones, L. (1980). *Great expectations.* New York: Coward, McCann & Geoghegan Publishers.

Kauffman, D. (1976). *Futurism and future studies.* Washington, D.C.: NEA.

Khatena, J. (1982). *Educational psychology of the gifted.* New York: John Wiley and Sons.

LaConte, R. (1984). Restructuring the curriculum. *Forum magazine,* May, 1984, p.18-19.

Maker, J. (1982). *Curriculum development for the gifted.* Rockville, MD: Aspen Publications.

Mead, M. (1970). *Culture and commitment.* Garden City, NY: Anchor Press/Doubleday.

Pirages, D. (1978). *The new context for international relations: Global eco-politics.* Duxbury Press, Belmont, CA.

Polak, F. (1973). *The image of the future.* (ed. & trans. by Elise Boulding), New York: Jossey-Bass.

Taylor, P. (1982). *The kids' whole catalog to the future.* New York: Random House.

Toffler, A. (1974). *Learning for tomorrow.* New York, NY: Random House.

Toffler, A. (1974). *Future shock.* New York: Bantam Books.

Toffler, A. (1981). *The third wave.* New York: Bantam Books.

Torrance, E.P. (1977). Today's students' images of the future. *Creative thinking,* Bellingham, WA: Western Washington University.

Whaley, C. (1984). *Future studies: Personal and global possibilities.* New York: Trillium Press.

Whaley, C., Whaley, H. (1986). *Future images: Futures studies for grades 4-12.* New York: Trillium Press.

Whaley, C. (1989) *Recycle Florida: A curriculum unit on the merits of recycling and environmental stewardship.* Waste Management, N.A., Inc./Leon County Schools, Tallahassee, FL.